TOUCHPOINTS™
for New Believers

Books in the
TOUCHPOINTS™
Series

TOUCHPOINTS

TOUCHPOINTS
for Women

TOUCHPOINTS
for Men

TOUCHPOINTS
for Students

TOUCHPOINTS
for Leaders

TOUCHPOINTS
for Recovery

TOUCHPOINTS
for New Believers

TOUCHPOINTS
Heaven

TouchPoints™
FOR NEW BELIEVERS

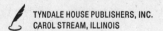

TYNDALE HOUSE PUBLISHERS, INC.
CAROL STREAM, ILLINOIS

Visit Tyndale's exciting website at www.tyndale.com.

TYNDALE, New Living Translation, NLT, the New Living Translation logo, and Tyndale's quill logo are registered trademarks of Tyndale House Publishers, Inc.

TouchPoints is a trademark of Tyndale House Publishers, Inc.

TouchPoints for New Believers

Copyright © 2009 by Ronald A. Beers. All rights reserved.

Designed by Jennifer Ghionzoli

General editor: Jason D. Beers
Contributing writers: Ronald A. Beers, Rebecca Beers, Brian R. Coffey, Jonathan Farrar, Jonathan Gray, Sean A. Harrison, Sandy Hull, Amy E. Mason, Rhonda K. O'Brien, Douglas J. Rumford, Linda Taylor

Scripture quotations are taken from the *Holy Bible*, New Living Translation, copyright © 1996, 2004, 2007 by Tyndale House Foundation. Used by permission of Tyndale House Publishers, Inc., Carol Stream, Illinois 60188. All rights reserved.

ISBN 978-1-4143-2022-9

Printed in the United States of America

17 16 15 14 13 12 11
 9   8   7   6   5   4   3

CONTENTS

ABILITIES

Where do my abilities come from, and how should I use them?

MATTHEW 25:29 | *To those who use well what they are given, even more will be given, and they will have an abundance. But from those who do nothing, even what little they have will be taken away.*

ROMANS 12:6 | *In his grace, God has given us different gifts for doing certain things well. So if God has given you . . . ability . . . [use it] with as much faith as God has given you.*

The natural abilities you have are gifts from God, and they are often a clue to what God wants you to do with your life. Why would God give you certain talents and spiritual gifts and then not ask you to use them? You may have natural gifts in the areas of sports, music, teaching, crafts, public speaking, or some other area. Use whatever gifts you have been given to bring honor and glory to God, and you will be right where you need to be to discover God's will for you.

ABSOLUTES

Are there absolutes in life, and how can I know what they are?

JUDGES 21:25 | *In those days Israel had no king; all the people did whatever seemed right in their own eyes.*

PROVERBS 12:19 | *Truthful words stand the test of time, but lies are soon exposed.*

ISAIAH 40:8 | *The grass withers and the flowers fade, but the word of our God stands forever.*

ROMANS 3:4 | *Even if everyone else is a liar, God is true. As the Scriptures say about him, "You will be proved right in what you say, and you will win your case in court."*

2 TIMOTHY 3:16 | *All Scripture is inspired by God and is useful to teach us what is true and to make us realize what is wrong in our lives. It corrects us when we are wrong and teaches us to do what is right.*

The Bible makes it clear that absolutes do exist and that absolute truth begins with God. It reveals the truths that make the world work, that make relationships work, and that determine your future. By studying these truths, you discover the way life works best. God's truth sets you free from a meaningless and chaotic life to one that has purpose today; has a certain and eternal future; and can always be fair and full of joy. That is truth others will want to follow.

What are some of the absolutes of the Christian faith?

ACTS 2:24-25, 31 | *God released [Jesus] from the horrors of death and raised him back to life, for death could not keep him in its grip. King David said this about him: "I see that the LORD is always with me." . . . David was looking into the future and speaking of the Messiah's resurrection. He was saying that God would not leave him among the dead or allow his body to rot in the grave.*

1 CORINTHIANS 15:4-6, 20 | *[Christ] was buried, and he was raised from the dead on the third day, just as the Scriptures said. He was seen by Peter and then by the Twelve. After that, he was seen by more than 500 of his followers at one time, most of whom are still alive, though some have died. . . . Christ has been raised from the dead. He is the first of a great harvest of all who have died.*

The resurrection of Jesus Christ is an absolute truth of the Christian faith. Because he was raised from the dead, he has conquered death, and therefore his promise of eternal life to all who have faith in him is certain.

JOHN 3:16 | *God loved the world so much that he gave his one and only Son, so that everyone who believes in him will not perish but have eternal life.*

JOHN 11:25-26 | *Jesus [said], "I am the resurrection and the life. Anyone who believes in me will live, even after dying. Everyone who lives in me and believes in me will never ever die."*

JOHN 14:6 | *Jesus [said], "I am the way, the truth, and the life. No one can come to the Father except through me."*

ROMANS 3:22, 30 | *We are made right with God by placing our faith in Jesus Christ. And this is true for everyone who believes, no matter who we are. . . . There is only one God, and he makes people right with himself only by faith, whether they are Jews or Gentiles.*

ROMANS 6:23 | *The wages of sin is death, but the free gift of God is eternal life through Christ Jesus our Lord.*

There is only one way for a person to enjoy eternal life with God in heaven. You can obtain this gift, called salvation, from God by believing that Jesus Christ died for your sins, by confessing your sins to Jesus so that you are forgiven for them, and by deciding that he is your one and only Lord.

ACTS 2:38-39 | *Each of you must repent of your sins and turn to God, and be baptized in the name of Jesus Christ for the forgiveness of your sins. Then you will receive the gift of the Holy Spirit. This promise is to you.*

The presence of God's Holy Spirit is an absolute guarantee to those who believe in Jesus Christ as their Lord. The Holy Spirit gives you the strength and power to avoid Satan's temptations and to live for God.

EXODUS 20:1-4, 7-8, 12-17 | *God gave the people all these instructions: "I am the LORD your God, who rescued you from the land of Egypt, the place of your slavery. You must not have any other god but me. You must not make for yourself an idol of any kind. . . . You must not misuse the name of the LORD your God. . . . Remember to observe the Sabbath day by keeping it holy. . . . Honor your father and mother. . . . You must not murder. You must not commit adultery. You must not steal.*

You must not testify falsely against your neighbor. You must not covet your neighbor's house. You must not covet your neighbor's wife, male or female servant, ox or donkey, or anything else that belongs to your neighbor."

God gave us the Ten Commandments. They are absolute truths that apply to all people in all cultures for all time. Obeying these commandments will point your life in the right direction, make your life more fulfilling and satisfying, save you from much harm, and keep your focus on God, the only One who can grant you eternal life.

NUMBERS 23:19 | *God is not a man, so he does not lie. He is not human, so he does not change his mind. Has he ever spoken and failed to act? Has he ever promised and not carried it through?*

1 CHRONICLES 16:34 | *Give thanks to the LORD, for he is good! His faithful love endures forever.*

PSALM 147:5 | *How great is our Lord! His power is absolute! His understanding is beyond comprehension!*

MALACHI 3:6 | *I am the LORD, and I do not change.*

ROMANS 8:38-39 | *Nothing can ever separate us from God's love. Neither death nor life, neither angels nor demons, neither our fears for today nor our worries about tomorrow—not even the powers of hell can separate us from God's love. No power in the sky above or in the earth below—indeed, nothing in all creation will ever be able to separate us from the love of God that is revealed in Christ Jesus our Lord.*

HEBREWS 13:8 | *Jesus Christ is the same yesterday, today, and forever.*

JAMES 1:17 | *Whatever is good and perfect comes down to us from God our Father, who created all the lights in the heavens. He never changes or casts a shifting shadow.*

God's character is unchanging. God is consistently all-powerful, absolutely good, the originator of truth, all-wise, and always faithful. And he loves you unconditionally.

ACTS 13:38-39 | *Through this man Jesus there is forgiveness for your sins. Everyone who believes in him is declared right with God.*

1 JOHN 1:9 | *If we confess our sins to him, he is faithful and just to forgive us our sins and to cleanse us.*

God's forgiveness is absolute. When God forgives you, it is forever. He never takes it back.

ACCEPTANCE

I feel so unworthy—does God really accept me?

ROMANS 5:8 | *God showed his great love for us by sending Christ to die for us while we were still sinners.*

ROMANS 8:39 | *Nothing . . . will ever be able to separate us from the love of God that is revealed in Christ Jesus our Lord.*

1 JOHN 4:9-10 | *God showed how much he loved us by sending his one and only Son into the world so that we might have eternal life through him. This is real love—not that we loved God, but that he loved us and sent his Son as a sacrifice to take away our sins.*

You are accepted by God because he made you and created you in his image. Nothing you can do will cause God to love you more because he loves you completely. And nothing you do can cause God to love you less. In fact, God simply accepts you, and he loves you so much that he sent his own Son to die for you, to take on himself the punishment you deserve for your sins. He died in your place so you can be accepted into eternity with him.

ACCOUNTABILITY

Why is accountability important?

PSALM 26:2 | *Put me on trial, LORD, and cross-examine me. Test my motives and my heart.*

PROVERBS 27:6 | *Wounds from a sincere friend are better than many kisses from an enemy.*

ROMANS 14:7-9, 12 | *We don't live for ourselves or die for ourselves. If we live, it's to honor the Lord. And if we die, it's to honor the Lord. So whether we live or die, we belong to the Lord. Christ died and rose again for this very purpose—to be Lord both of the living and of the dead. . . . Each of us will give a personal account to God.*

The purpose of life, both now and forever, is to honor God. Who is helping you do that, and how do you know if you're doing it well? You need someone to keep you accountable. You also need God to hold you accountable. You don't want to wait until the end of life to find out from God if your life was lived well. Go to him now, by reading his Word, to make sure that your thoughts, words, and actions are in tune with his and honoring to him. And ask godly friends how you are doing. Accountability keeps you honest, joyful, and on the right path so that when you come face-to-face with God, you can be sure he will be pleased.

ADVERSITY/TROUBLE

Why does God allow troubles to come my way even after I've become a Christian?

ROMANS 5:3 | *We can rejoice, too, when we run into problems and trials, for we know that they help us develop endurance.*

JAMES 1:2-4 | *When troubles come your way, consider it an opportunity for great joy. For you know that when your faith is tested, your endurance has a chance to grow. So let it grow, for when your endurance is fully developed, you will be perfect and complete, needing nothing.*

The one thing you can count on about adversity is that it will come—the issue is what you will do when it arrives. Adversity is hard to understand, but there is evidence in life of its benefits: If you never got sick, your body would never develop the immunity to fight off greater diseases. In the same way, if God didn't build up your immunity to adversity, you would crumble under the powerful trouble that life and Satan bring. So when adversity comes, regardless of the source, always move quickly toward God and keep him in your sight. Then you will develop the strength to overcome it.

PHILIPPIANS 1:12-14 | *Everything that has happened to me here has helped to spread the Good News. For everyone here, including the whole palace guard, knows that I am in chains because of Christ. And because of my imprisonment, most of the believers here have gained confidence and boldly speak God's message without fear.*

God uses your circumstances to help you grow. Then you can help others grow. Anyone can be joyful and faithful when life is going well, but when life gets tough, believers have a unique opportunity to show how a relationship with God brings comfort, confidence, and hope.

Is God absent in my times of pain and trouble?

PSALM 9:10 | *Those who know your name trust in you, for you, O LORD, do not abandon those who search for you.*

PSALM 27:10 | *Even if my father and mother abandon me, the LORD will hold me close.*

When you accidentally cut yourself, you become completely focused on how bad it is and on how to stop the bleeding. In the same way, when you feel God has abandoned you, it is because you have become so focused on easing the pain of your problems that you have neglected God, forgetting that he has promised to help you in your difficulties. To abandon you, God would have to stop loving you, and he cannot do that, for he is love.

Although it is impossible to avoid all adversity, what are things I can do to avoid some of it?

PSALM 119:9 | *How can a young person stay pure? By obeying your word.*

PSALM 119:105 | *Your word is a lamp to guide my feet and a light for my path.*

The consequences of sin often bring unneeded adversity into your life. By obeying God's Word, you can avoid many kinds of adversity you might otherwise inflict on yourself.

PROVERBS 21:23 | *Watch your tongue and keep your mouth shut, and you will stay out of trouble.*

JAMES 3:2, 5-6 | *If we could control our tongues, we would be perfect and could also control ourselves in every other way. . . . The tongue is a small thing that makes grand speeches. But a tiny spark can set a great forest on fire. And the tongue is a flame of fire.*

Controlling your tongue can help you avoid adversity. Many times trouble can be avoided by being careful about what you say.

PROVERBS 15:19 | *A lazy person's way is blocked with briers, but the path of the upright is an open highway.*

Honest work can help avoid adversity.

PROVERBS 11:14 | *Without wise leadership, a nation falls; there is safety in having many advisers.*

PROVERBS 13:13 | *People who despise advice are asking for trouble; those who respect a command will succeed.*

Following advice from godly people will help you avoid trouble.

ANGER OF GOD

What makes God angry?

PSALM 7:10-11 | *God is my shield, saving those whose hearts are true and right. God is an honest judge. He is angry with the wicked every day.*

ROMANS 1:18 | *God shows his anger from heaven against all sinful, wicked people who suppress the truth by their wickedness.*

EPHESIANS 2:2-3 | *You used to live in sin, just like the rest of the world, obeying the devil—the commander of the powers in the unseen world. He is the spirit at work in the hearts of those who refuse to obey God. All of us used to live that way, following the passionate desires and inclinations of our sinful nature. By our very nature we were subject to God's anger, just like everyone else.*

God gets angry, but only for the right reasons. Because God is perfectly sinless and holy, he gets angry when you sin because he knows that sin hurts your relationship with him—it separates you from him. And it's only through a relationship with him that life can have meaning and purpose.

It is good that God gets angry at sin because that shows how much he longs to have a pure and perfect relationship with you. It is because of his anger at sin that he made a plan to get rid of it; then you can live forever in heaven with him, where there is no sin and no death.

APPROVAL

Do I have to earn God's approval?

ROMANS 3:27-28 | *Can we boast, then, that we have done anything to be accepted by God? No, because our acquittal is not based on obeying the law. It is based on faith. So we are made right with God through faith and not by obeying the law.*

GALATIANS 2:19 | *When I tried to keep the law, it condemned me. So I died to the law—I stopped trying to meet all its requirements—so that I might live for God.*

You cannot earn God's approval because he already approves of you! Your approval is not based on performance but on the fact that you are his creation. When you obey God, you are expressing your gratitude to God and love for him, not trying to win his approval.

ROMANS 3:23; 10:9 | *Everyone has sinned; we all fall short of God's glorious standard. . . . [But] if you confess with your mouth that Jesus is Lord and believe in your heart that God raised him from the dead, you will be saved.*

While God loves you unconditionally, he does not approve of your sinful behavior. When you understand that it is your sin that separates you from God and that Jesus died and rose again to take away your sin so you can be reconciled to God, you realize how much God values you. When, at the moment of salvation, you confess your sins to him, seek his forgiveness, and commit to following Jesus, you are approved to enter heaven for eternity. There's a difference between God's unconditional love for you (he doesn't love you more or less because you became a Christian) and his conditional salvation (he saves only those who admit they have sinned and need his forgiveness). Understanding that difference is a matter of life and death.

ASTROLOGY

Is astrology wrong?

EXODUS 20:3 | *You must not have any other god but me.*

DEUTERONOMY 18:10-11 | *Do not let your people practice fortune-telling, or use sorcery, or interpret omens, or engage in witch-craft, or cast spells, or function as mediums or psychics, or call forth the spirits of the dead.*

2 KINGS 21:6 | *Manasseh . . . sacrificed his own son in the fire. He practiced sorcery and divination, and he consulted with mediums and psychics. He did much that was evil in the LORD's sight, arousing his anger.*

Astrology is wrong because it worships the heavens instead of the God who created the heavens. And worshiping anything or anyone other than God is idolatry.

Can astrology give me direction?

GENESIS 1:16-17 | *God made two great lights—the larger one to govern the day, and the smaller one to govern the night. He also made the stars. God set these lights in the sky to light the earth.*

Don't seek advice from the stars, but from God, the Creator of the stars. Only he can give you direction for your life, because he created you, too. You should never worship the Creation instead of the Creator. *God* controls all celestial events, so only *he* can point you in the right direction.

BACKSLIDING

How can I avoid drifting away from God?

MATTHEW 26:41 | *Keep watch and pray, so that you will not give in to temptation. For the spirit is willing, but the body is weak!*

HEBREWS 2:1 | *We must listen very carefully to the truth we have heard, or we may drift away from it.*

Backsliding means taking a step backward in your spiritual walk with God, falling back into a sinful lifestyle or habit that weakens your relationship with him. Each time you backslide, you become more comfortable with the sinful habit you have given in to and your heart becomes a bit harder, making it more difficult to hear God calling you to come close to him. But each time you obey God's Word rather than disobey, each time you offer a prayer to God, and each time you remind yourself to be alert to temptation, you will take a step toward God rather than away. It sounds simple, but it takes discipline and practice to keep from backsliding.

BEGINNINGS

Is it really possible for me to get a fresh start?

2 CORINTHIANS 5:17 | *Anyone who belongs to Christ has become a new person. The old life is gone; a new life has begun!*

Do you have times when you long for a fresh start? God promises that when you place your faith in Jesus, you get a new beginning because his forgiveness washes your sins away, giving you a clean heart before God. Then God promises to put his Holy Spirit in your clean heart (see Acts 2:38) and give you the strength, power, and wisdom to live the way God created you to live. And when you mess up, God's forgiveness always provides the opportunity to begin again, any day and any time.

BEHAVIOR

Why is godly behavior important?

MATTHEW 5:16 | *Let your good deeds shine out for all to see, so that everyone will praise your heavenly Father.*

LUKE 11:28 | *Blessed are all who hear the word of God and put it into practice.*

ROMANS 13:13 | *Don't participate in the darkness of wild parties and drunkenness, or in sexual promiscuity and immoral living, or in quarreling and jealousy.*

Faith alone is enough for salvation, but the evidence that your faith is genuine is seen through your behavior. If your faith doesn't change your sinful behavior, then was your confession of faith really genuine when you asked God to forgive your sins, enter your life, and transform who you are? When people see godly behavior in you, they will want to know what makes you different. You then have a wonderful opportunity to tell them, and God promises blessings when you do.

BELIEF

Why is it so important to believe in Jesus?

JOHN 3:36 | *Anyone who believes in God's Son has eternal life.*

Believing in Jesus gives you hope—today, tomorrow, and for eternity. You have hope for today because his forgiveness transforms relationships. You have hope for tomorrow because he promises to work in your life to make you all he created you to be. You have hope for eternity because he promises that you will live forever in heaven, where your body will be perfectly healthy and life will be meaningful, peaceful, and fulfilling.

BELONGING

How can I feel that I belong in the church?

ROMANS 12:4-6 | *Just as our bodies have many parts and each part has a special function, so it is with Christ's body. We are many parts of one body, and we all belong to each other. In his grace, God has given us different gifts for doing certain things well. So if God has given you . . . ability, . . . [use it] with as much faith as God has given you.*

Belonging to God makes you part of Christ's body, the church. Now you need to figure out what part of the body you are. A hand? A foot? Ears? Eyes? When you discover what "part" you are, you have discovered your spiritual gift. And when you use that gift as God intended, you find your place of belonging in the church, where you can best serve God and others and where you feel a sense of purpose and fulfillment. When each person in the body understands what his or her part is, then the body functions as it should and all members feel like they belong.

BIBLE

Why should I read the Bible?

2 TIMOTHY 3:16-17 | *All Scripture is inspired by God and is useful to teach us what is true and to make us realize what is wrong in our lives. It corrects us when we are wrong and teaches us to do what is right. God uses it to prepare and equip his people to do every good work.*

How remarkable that the God of the universe would actually want to communicate with us! We are creatures of a material, physical world to which we relate through our five senses. God is a spiritual being. We in our physical state cannot see him, hear him, or touch him, so how can he communicate with us? Through the Bible. Over several centuries, God inspired a select number of people to write down what we needed to know about him and what we must do now in order to live forever with him in heaven.

These writings have been collected into a book called the Holy Bible—holy because it contains the sacred words of almighty God. In a miraculous way, the Bible speaks to all of us in general and to each of us individually. Its truths apply across generations, across cultures, and across life experience because it was written by the One who created life itself. Anyone buying a computer receives a thick owner's manual. Most of us read just enough to allow us to get it up and running, to perform the basic tasks for which we have acquired it. But if we want to thoroughly understand the computer—all it is capable of—we must read the entire manual. Most of us will never do this, and so we miss out on what the computer has to offer. Just as with the computer manual, most of us read only enough of the Bible to get by. Consequently, we miss much that God's Word has to offer. We need to read God's Word daily so we can thoroughly understand all God wants us to know.

How can a book written so long ago be relevant for me today?

ISAIAH 40:8 | *The grass withers and the flowers fade, but the word of our God stands forever.*

HEBREWS 4:12 | *The word of God is alive and powerful. It is sharper than the sharpest two-edged sword, cutting between soul and spirit, between joint and marrow. It exposes our innermost thoughts and desires.*

Because the Bible is the Word of God, it is the only document that is "living"— relevant for all people in all places in any time period. People change over time, but their basic needs for love, acceptance, purpose, and fulfillment remain the same. The Bible addresses all human needs. It is as contemporary as the heart of God and as relevant as your most urgent need, sustaining you and bringing you joy no matter what happens in life, because God is speaking to you through it.

Can I truly trust the Bible as God's Word?

PSALM 18:30 | *God's way is perfect. All the LORD's promises prove true.*

2 PETER 1:20-21 | *No prophecy in Scripture ever came from the prophet's own understanding. . . . No, those prophets were moved by the Holy Spirit, and they spoke from God.*

The Bible has stood the test of time better than any other document in human history. It has been faithfully preserved because it is God's very words to us, and he will not let them disappear from the face of the earth or its truths be altered by human hands in any way.

How often should I read the Bible?

DEUTERONOMY 6:6 | *You must commit yourselves wholeheartedly to these commands that I am giving you today.*

JOSHUA 1:8 | *Study this Book of Instruction continually. Meditate on it day and night so you will be sure to obey everything written in it. Only then will you prosper and succeed in all you do.*

The Bible is for regular reading and meditation in order to learn about God and communicate with him. If at all possible, this should be done daily. When God says "meditate on it day and night," he doesn't mean reading the Bible just when you get around to it.

What will I experience when I read the Bible?

PSALM 19:8 | *The commandments of the LORD are right, bringing joy to the heart. The commands of the LORD are clear, giving insight for living.*

PSALM 119:54 | *Your decrees have been the theme of my songs wherever I have lived.*

PSALM 119:130 | *The teaching of your word gives light, so even the simple can understand.*

PSALM 119:162 | *I rejoice in your word like one who discovers a great treasure.*

Reading the Bible helps you experience joy, insight, wisdom, and knowledge and find the keys to living. This happens when you have an open mind while reading the Bible, listening to thoughts that are sparked by the Holy Spirit.

JOHN 8:32 | *You will know the truth, and the truth will set you free.*

Reading the Bible tells you how to be set free from sin.

ACTS 17:11 | *The people of Berea were more open-minded than those in Thessalonica, and they listened eagerly to Paul's message. They searched the Scriptures day after day to see if Paul and Silas were teaching the truth.*

Reading the Bible teaches you how to recognize true and false doctrine when you hear it.

DEUTERONOMY 17:20 | *This regular reading will prevent him from becoming proud and acting as if he is above his fellow citizens.*

Reading the Bible helps you keep a right attitude toward God and others.

PSALM 19:11 | *[The laws of the Lord] are a warning to your servant.*

PSALM 119:24 | *Your laws please me; they give me wise advice.*

Reading the Bible warns you about things that will harm you and provides good counsel for your problems.

PSALM 119:9 | *How can a young person stay pure? By obeying your word.*

PSALM 119:105 | *Your word is a lamp to guide my feet and a light for my path.*

Reading the Bible guides you in daily living and helps you stay closer to God.

PSALM 119:50 | *Your promise revives me; it comforts me in all my troubles.*

Reading the Bible gives you encouragement and comfort.

How do I know when my understanding of the Bible is right?

MATTHEW 13:23 | *The seed that fell on good soil represents those who truly hear and understand God's word and produce a harvest of thirty, sixty, or even a hundred times as much as had been planted!*

COLOSSIANS 1:6 | *This same Good News that came to you . . . is bearing fruit everywhere by changing lives, just as it changed your lives from the day you first heard and understood the truth.*

You know you have understood rightly when the truth bears fruit in your life. In other words, true understanding of Scripture leads to transformed living.

PROVERBS 10:31 | *The mouth of the godly person gives wise advice.*

PROVERBS 15:7 | *The lips of the wise give good advice.*

If you are not sure what a certain Scripture means, ask your pastor or another Christian who knows the Bible well, or refer to a study guide or commentary on the book or passage that is confusing to you.

BODY OF CHRIST

What is the body of Christ?

1 CORINTHIANS 12:12-13 | *The human body has many parts, but the many parts make up one whole body. So it is with the body of Christ. Some of us are Jews, some are Gentiles, some are slaves, and some are free. But we have all been baptized into one body by one Spirit, and we all share the same Spirit.*

EPHESIANS 1:23 | *The church is [Christ's] body; it is made full and complete by Christ, who fills all things everywhere with himself.*

EPHESIANS 4:11-12 | *These are the gifts Christ gave to the church: the apostles, the prophets, the evangelists, and the pastors and teachers. Their responsibility is to equip God's people to do his work and build up the church, the body of Christ.*

The body of Christ simply refers to all people around the world who believe in Jesus Christ as their Savior and Lord, who have received his forgiveness from sin. The body of Christ is also called the church.

What is my role in the body of Christ?

ROMANS 12:4-6 | *Just as our bodies have many parts and each part has a special function, so it is with Christ's body. We are many parts of one body, and we all belong to each other. In his grace, God has given us different gifts for doing certain things well.*

EPHESIANS 4:16 | *He makes the whole body fit together perfectly. As each part does its own special work, it helps the other parts grow, so that the whole body is healthy and growing and full of love.*

God assigns a variety of servant roles based on the abilities he gives people and the needs of his church. It is important for you to discover the special and specific gifts God has created in you and to learn how to use those gifts to serve him.

BOREDOM

Isn't being a Christian boring?

HEBREWS 6:11-12 | *Our great desire is that you will keep on loving others as long as life lasts, in order to make certain that what you hope for will come true. Then you will not become spiritually dull and indifferent. Instead, you will follow the example of those who are going to inherit God's promises because of their faith and endurance.*

Being a Christian can seem boring to many—"Don't do this"; "You can't do that." But those who grasp what the Christian life is all about find it full and exciting. When you realize that almighty God wants to work through you to accomplish some of his work in the world, you will be amazed to see the great things he could accomplish through you. Focus on using and developing your God-given gifts, as well as on the eternal rewards God promises to believers, and your life will be continually exciting. If you become bored in your Christian life, it is because you are not making yourself available to God and asking him to pour his blessings through you onto others.

CALL OF GOD

How do I know what my calling is?

PSALM 119:105 | *Your word is a lamp to guide my feet and a light for my path.*

The first step in knowing your calling is to get to know God better by reading his Word. As God communicates to you through the Bible, he will show you what to do and where he wants you to go.

DANIEL 1:17 | *God gave these four young men an unusual aptitude for understanding every aspect of literature and wisdom. And God gave Daniel the special ability to interpret the meanings of visions and dreams.*

God has given every individual special aptitudes and abilities. These provide the biggest clue to what God wants you to do. When he calls you to do something unique for him, he will almost always allow you to use your God-given gifts to get the job done. In the meantime, develop those special abilities and begin to use them. In God's timing, you will see what he wants you to do.

ACTS 20:24 | *[Paul said,] "My life is worth nothing to me unless I use it for finishing the work assigned me by the Lord Jesus."*

When God gives you a specific calling, it fills your thoughts and energies so that you have a longing to pursue it wholeheartedly.

ROMANS 12:2 | *Let God transform you into a new person by changing the way you think. Then you will learn to know God's will for you, which is good and pleasing and perfect.*

When you let God transform you by the power of his Holy Spirit, he will literally begin to change the way you think so you will know what he wants you to do.

Has God called me to do specific things?

JEREMIAH 1:4-5 | *The LORD gave me this message: "I knew you before I formed you in your mother's womb. Before you were born I set you apart and appointed you as my prophet to the nations."*

God may call you to do a certain job or to accomplish a very specific task. When that happens, he will make sure you know what it is. You will feel a very strong sense of leading from him. It's up to you to respond and walk through the door of opportunity he opens.

1 CORINTHIANS 12:4, 7 | *There are different kinds of spiritual gifts, but the same Spirit is the source of them all. . . . A spiritual gift is given to each of us so we can help each other.*

God gives each individual a spiritual gift (sometimes more than one!) and a special ministry in the church. You can use your gifts to help and encourage others and to bring glory to God's name. These specific spiritual gifts help you fulfill the purpose for which he made you.

1 CORINTHIANS 7:17 | *Each of you should continue to live in whatever situation the Lord has placed you, and remain as you were when God first called you.*

The call to follow Jesus does not necessarily mean a call to a specific job or Christian ministry. Sometimes your call may simply be to obey God wherever you are right now.

ECCLESIASTES 11:9 | *Do everything you want to do; take it all in. But remember that you must give an account to God for everything you do.*

God gives you the freedom to follow many different roads over the course of life and pursue many different activities, but remember that you will have to answer to him for everything you do. Not everything you do is a call from God, but everything you do is accountable to God.

CARE/CARING

Does God really care what happens to me?

PSALM 31:7 | *I will be glad and rejoice in your unfailing love, for you have seen my troubles, and you care about the anguish of my soul.*

PSALM 71:6 | *[O Lord,] you have been with me from birth; from my mother's womb you have cared for me. No wonder I am always praising you!*

God's love for you began before you were born, continues throughout your life, and extends through eternity. Since he created you to have a relationship with him, he cares about every detail of your life. He knows all your troubles and hurts, and he longs to take care of you during the difficult times in your life.

CAUTION

What are some areas in which I should exercise caution?

JOSHUA 23:11 | *Be very careful to love the LORD your God.*

HEBREWS 3:12 | *Be careful then, dear brothers and sisters. Make sure that your own hearts are not evil and unbelieving, turning you away from the living God.*

Be careful not to let anything distract you from whole-hearted devotion to God. Be cautious about anything in life that has the potential to damage your relationship with him.

DEUTERONOMY 4:9 | *Watch out! Be careful never to forget what you yourself have seen. Do not let these memories escape from your mind as long as you live! And be sure to pass them on.*

DEUTERONOMY 8:10-11 | *When you have eaten your fill, be sure to praise the LORD your God. . . . Beware that in your plenty you do not forget the LORD your God and disobey his commands.*

Be careful to remember all God has done for you in the past so you don't become proud in the present and forget to rely on him for your future.

HEBREWS 2:1 | *We must listen very carefully to the truth we have heard, or we may drift away from it.*

Be careful to focus on the truths you read in Scripture and hear from godly teachers. When you don't focus on the road as you drive, you are at risk of drifting and putting your life in great danger. In the same way, when you don't focus on God's Word, you are in danger of drifting off the road that leads to a safe and happy destination. Your spiritual life will be in danger.

MARK 14:38 | *Keep watch and pray, so that you will not give in to temptation. For the spirit is willing, but the body is weak.*

1 CORINTHIANS 10:12-13 | *If you think you are standing strong, be careful not to fall. The temptations in your life are no different from what others experience. And God is faithful. He will not allow the temptation to be more than you can stand. When you are tempted, he will show you a way out so that you can endure.*

1 PETER 5:8 | *Stay alert! Watch out for your great enemy, the devil. He prowls around like a roaring lion, looking for someone to devour.*

Be careful about temptation. Satan is constantly on the attack, trying to tempt you to sin against God. You will give in from time to time—every human does. But caution will cause you to be aware of when you are giving in so that you can recognize it, admit it, and correct it. When you throw caution to the wind, you give in to temptation at every whim, and you are in danger of being completely ineffective for God.

PROVERBS 4:23 | *Guard your heart above all else, for it determines the course of your life.*

Be careful to guard your heart because it is the center of your desires and affections. Your heart is especially vulnerable because it is easily swayed by emotion and sometimes is not rational. If you are caught up with emotion, your heart will urge you to do whatever it takes to keep those feelings alive and on fire, even if those actions lead you to do something that could destroy you.

PROVERBS 22:7 | *Just as the rich rule the poor, so the borrower is servant to the lender.*

HEBREWS 13:5 | *Don't love money; be satisfied with what you have.*

Be careful in handling your money. More than almost anything in life, money can cause damage to relationships and compromise your values.

PROVERBS 20:18 | *Plans succeed through good counsel; don't go to war without wise advice.*

Be careful in giving and receiving advice. Receiving the right advice makes you wiser; giving the wrong advice can cause others to stumble.

JAMES 3:5-8 | *The tongue is a small thing that makes grand speeches. But a tiny spark can set a great forest on fire. . . . It can set your whole life on fire. . . . People can tame all kinds of animals, birds, reptiles, and fish, but no one can tame the tongue. It is restless and evil, full of deadly poison.*

Be careful with your words, for they reveal your character. They have the power to build others up or tear them down.

CELEBRATION

Is celebration okay in God's eyes?

DEUTERONOMY 16:14-15 | *This festival will be a happy time of celebrating with your sons and daughters . . . to honor the*

LORD your God . . . for it is he who blesses you with bountiful harvests and gives you success in all your work.

MATTHEW 25:23 | *The master said, "Well done, my good and faithful servant. You have been faithful in handling this small amount, so now I will give you many more responsibilities. Let's celebrate together!"*

The Bible teaches that celebration is both important and necessary. Celebration gives you the opportunity to savor the joy of work, to experience the satisfaction of accomplishment, and to enjoy the good things of Creation. It fosters a spirit of gratitude and renews your energy for the work that still must be done.

CERTAINTY

How can I know there is a God?

ECCLESIASTES 3:11 | *God has made everything beautiful for its own time. He has planted eternity in the human heart, but even so, people cannot see the whole scope of God's work from beginning to end.*

ROMANS 1:19-20 | *[People] know the truth about God because he has made it obvious to them. For ever since the world was created, people have seen the earth and sky. Through everything God made, they can clearly see his invisible qualities—his eternal power and divine nature. So they have no excuse for not knowing God.*

ROMANS 2:14-15 | *Even Gentiles, who do not have God's written law, show that they know his law when they instinctively obey it, even without having heard it. They demonstrate that God's law is written in their hearts, for their own conscience and thoughts either accuse them or tell them they are doing right.*

If God does not exist, then why is everyone—Christians, atheists, agnostics, and so forth—still talking about him? It is because our inner conscience wants to point somewhere to explain the world. God has built a conscience into every human being so that we will never forget him. Listening to one's conscience begins a search that will lead to God.

GENESIS 1:3, 11, 14, 20, 24, 26 | *God said, "Let there be light."* . . . *Then God said, "Let the land sprout with vegetation—every sort of seed-bearing plant, and trees that grow seed-bearing fruit."* . . . *Then God said, "Let lights appear in the sky to separate the day from the night. Let them be signs to mark the seasons, days, and years."* . . . *Then God said, "Let the waters swarm with fish and other life. Let the skies be filled with birds of every kind."* . . . *Then God said, "Let the earth produce every sort of animal."* . . . *Then God said, "Let us make human beings."*

PSALM 19:1-2, 4-6 | *The heavens proclaim the glory of God. The skies display his craftsmanship. Day after day they continue to speak; night after night they make him known.* . . . *Their message has gone throughout the earth, and their words to all the world. God has made a home in the heavens for the sun. It bursts forth like a radiant bridegroom after his wedding. It rejoices like a great athlete eager to run the race. The sun rises at one end of the heavens and follows its course to the other end. Nothing can hide from its heat.*

You can know that there is a God by looking at the design of nature. All Creation testifies to the Creator. Nothing can be made without a maker. The vastness of the universe—now believed to contain at least one hundred billion galaxies, each with one hundred billion stars—reveals a God who is powerful. The complexity of life—the hundreds of amino acids needed to form a protein molecule and the hundreds of protein molecules needed to form one cell and the miraculous double-helix DNA molecule that encodes all the information necessary for living cells to be maintained and reproduced—points to a God who is intelligent beyond human understanding. The multitude of forces, elements, and precise conditions necessary for life to exist on earth points not to a cosmic accident but to a God who deliberately created the world, and created it for a reason—to enter into a relationship with his created beings. Creation speaks of a God who is both infinitely powerful and infinitely loving.

DANIEL 4:27, 30-31, 33-35, 37 | *[Daniel said,] "King Nebuchadnezzar, please accept my advice. Stop sinning and do what is right. Break from your wicked past." . . . As [Nebuchadnezzar] looked out across the city, he said, "Look at this great city of Babylon! By my own mighty power, I have built this beautiful city . . . to display my majestic splendor." While these words were still in his mouth, a voice called down from heaven, "O King Nebuchadnezzar, . . . you are no longer ruler of this kingdom." . . . That same hour the judgment was fulfilled, and Nebuchadnezzar was driven from human society. He ate grass like a cow, and he . . . lived this way until his hair was as long as eagles' feathers and his nails were like birds' claws. "After this time had passed, I, Nebuchadnezzar, looked up to heaven. My sanity returned, and I praised and worshiped the Most High and honored the one who lives forever. His rule is everlasting, and his kingdom is eternal. All the people of the earth are nothing compared to him. . . . Now I, Nebuchadnezzar, praise and glorify and honor the King of heaven. All his acts are just and true, and he is able to humble the proud."*

You can know that there is a God through listening to the testimony of others. When God changes lives, it is clear that a divine miracle has occurred.

ISAIAH 41:20 | *I am doing this so all who see this miracle will understand what it means—that it is the LORD who has done this, the Holy One of Israel who created it.*

ISAIAH 46:8-11 | *Do not forget this! Keep it in mind! . . . Remember the things I have done in the past. For I alone am God! . . . Only I can tell you the future before it even happens. Everything I plan will come to pass. . . . I have said what I would do, and I will do it.*

You can know there is a God through the fulfillment of prophecy. The track record of the prophets, who spoke long before the prophesied events, confirms that what they spoke was truth—God's truth.

How can I be sure of my salvation?

JOHN 6:37 | *[Jesus said,] "Those the Father has given me will come to me, and I will never reject them."*

Your confidence should be rooted in God's hold on you, not your grip on God. When you give your life to him, he will hold you and never let go. You can approach God knowing that he gladly welcomes you and will never reject you. He will never say, "Sorry, I don't have time for you," or "Please don't bother me right now." You can be assured that God always listens, always hears, always loves, is always there.

CHANCE

Does God control everything? How much of life is chance?

ISAIAH 45:18 | *The LORD is God, and he created the heavens and earth and put everything in place. He made the world to be lived in, not to be a place of empty chaos. "I am the LORD," he says, "and there is no other."*

JEREMIAH 29:11 | *"I know the plans I have for you," says the LORD. "They are plans for good and not for disaster, to give you a future and a hope."*

EPHESIANS 1:10 | *This is [God's] plan: At the right time he will bring everything together under the authority of Christ— everything in heaven and on earth.*

While some things just happen, much of what determines the direction of your life is part of God's plan for you. God opens doors of opportunity, but you must walk through them. If all things happened merely by chance, it would point to either no God at all or a God who is impersonal and detached from the human race. What a depressing and hopeless view of life that would be! However, the Bible says that God is compassionate and deeply involved in his creation, so much so that he has an eternal plan for it and for you. While you may not understand how certain life events fit into God's perfect plan, you can be confident that God is watching over your life and guiding you in a specific direction.

GENESIS 42:21 | *Speaking among themselves, [Joseph's brothers] said, "Clearly we are being punished because of what we did to Joseph long ago. We saw his anguish when he pleaded for his life, but we wouldn't listen. That's why we're in this trouble."*

ECCLESIASTES 2:17-19 | *I came to hate life because everything done here under the sun is so troubling. Everything is meaningless— like chasing the wind. I came to hate all my hard work here on earth, for I must leave to others everything I have earned. And who can tell whether my successors will be wise or foolish? Yet they will control everything I have gained by my skill and hard work under the sun. How meaningless!*

When faced with a confusing, random, or chaotic circumstance, you try to determine what happened and why, to find any reason that might bring order or understanding to the situation. Sometimes there is no good reason—it just happened because you live in a sinful, fallen world where bad things affect both good and bad people. But often there is a reason. Sin comes back to haunt everyone, even sins committed long ago, because harmful actions always cause harmful reactions. God may be disciplining you, or he may be trying to teach you something. Before you just write off an event to chance, ask yourself if something you did might have caused this. Ask yourself what God might be trying to teach you and what you might learn from it. Then ask him to help you move on with a fresh start.

CHANGE

I don't like change. How do I deal with it?

MARK 4:2-3, 20 | *[Jesus] taught [the people] by telling many stories in the form of parables, such as this one: "Listen! A farmer went out to plant some seed. . . . The seed that fell on good soil represents those who hear and accept God's word and produce a harvest of thirty, sixty, or even a hundred times as much as had been planted!"*

ACTS 3:19 | *Repent of your sins and turn to God, so that your sins may be wiped away.*

JAMES 1:17 | *God our Father, who created all the lights in the heavens, . . . never changes or casts a shifting shadow.*

Change is one of the great constants of life. Whether because of the slow and gradual erosion of time or the swift and cataclysmic moments of trauma, change happens to everything and everyone. People change, relationships change, jobs change, technology changes—indeed life itself can be described as a process of continual change. Some changes are positive: a new friend, a new house, a financial windfall. Others are negative: a tragic loss, a job layoff, the upheaval of natural disaster. Either way, change can be stressful. The Bible teaches two great truths about change. The first is that despite the changing world around us, God is changeless and dependable. The second is that God calls for an inner change of heart, called *repentance*, that produces an outward change of lifestyle, called *obedience*. When you change your heart, you will change your life forever.

Does God ever change?

LAMENTATIONS 5:19 | *LORD, you remain the same forever! Your throne continues from generation to generation.*

MALACHI 3:6 | *I am the LORD, and I do not change.*

HEBREWS 13:8 | *Jesus Christ is the same yesterday, today, and forever.*

The character of God is unchanging and thus completely reliable. This is good news, because no matter how much your life changes, no matter what new situations you face, God goes with you and you can always count on his promise to help, guide, and care for you.

1 PETER 1:4 | *We have a priceless inheritance—an inheritance that is kept in heaven for you, pure and undefiled, beyond the reach of change and decay.*

Since God and his Word never change, his promises never change either! This gives you assurance that eternal life in heaven is a reality and that it will be as wonderful as the Bible says.

CHARACTER

Why should I be concerned about developing character? Don't I have only a few years on earth, and shouldn't I enjoy them as much as possible?

MATTHEW 5:8 | *God blesses those whose hearts are pure, for they will see God.*

The error is often one of perspective—you believe that temporary thrills and pleasures will make you happy. However, you end up chasing these things repeatedly because they never satisfy you. They leave you empty and only wanting more in order to make you feel good. In contrast, God's Word clues you in on the source of true, lasting happiness. When you live as the Bible teaches, you become full of joy because those choices literally change your perspective. Try it—you will not be disappointed. The testimonies of countless changed lives prove it.

Why does character matter?

EZEKIEL 18:5-9 | *Suppose a certain man is righteous and does what is just and right. . . . He does not commit adultery. . . . He is a merciful creditor. . . . He does not rob the poor but instead gives food to the hungry and provides clothes for the needy. He grants loans without interest, stays away from injustice, is honest and fair when judging others, and faithfully obeys my decrees and regulations. Anyone who does these things is just and will surely live, says the Sovereign LORD.*

People often argue that their personal lives do not matter as long as they perform well on the job or look good in public. God, however, does not make a distinction between public and private life. Justice, righteousness, integrity, mercy, honesty, fairness, and faithfulness are essential traits of a godly person's character because they reflect what God wants a person to be. Such traits also demonstrate an understanding of what is truly important in life—loving, honoring, and respecting God and others.

Can't I work on my character when I get older?

1 TIMOTHY 4:12 | *Don't let anyone think less of you because you are young. Be an example to all believers in what you say, in the way you live, in your love, your faith, and your purity.*

You don't know how long you will live. But more important, your character is simply a reflection of who you are. If you aren't interested in developing godly character now, you probably won't be interested in it later because the older you become, the harder it is to change your thoughts and convictions. Why not start to live the fulfilling and dynamic life that God is promising you now?

CHOICES

How can I know that I am making good choices?

PSALM 25:12 | *Who are those who fear the LORD? He will show them the path they should choose.*

HOSEA 14:9 | *Let those who are wise understand these things. Let those with discernment listen carefully. The paths of the LORD are true and right, and righteous people live by walking in them. But in those paths sinners stumble and fall.*

You make many choices each day to follow something. Physically, you might follow diets, exercise programs, and fashion trends. Socially, you might follow role models, friends, and other people you admire. You spend your free time following TV shows, sports teams, and entertainment. But your most important choice is spiritual—should you follow God? Choosing to follow God is a wise choice since he created you and knows what's best for you. When you make the choice to follow God first, your other choices of whom or what to follow will be clarified by God's wisdom and vision for your life.

CHURCH

What is the purpose of the church? Why should I attend?

ACTS 2:47 | *Each day the Lord added to their fellowship those who were being saved.*

The physical church is a gathering place for those who are saved by faith in Christ. Your attendance encourages other believers and strengthens the body of Christ.

1 CORINTHIANS 3:16-17 | *Don't you realize that all of you together are the temple of God and that the Spirit of God lives in you? . . . God's temple is holy, and you are that temple.*

God's church is not a physical building but the believers who gather inside the building. There the Holy Spirit teaches you, together with other Christians, how to truly change for good and influence others because of your changed lives.

EPHESIANS 4:11-12 | *These are the gifts Christ gave to the church: the apostles, the prophets, the evangelists, and the pastors and teachers. Their responsibility is to equip God's people to do his work and build up the church, the body of Christ.*

The church exists in part to teach and prepare God's people to do God's work and to encourage them in their faith.

1 CORINTHIANS 12:12-13 | *The human body has many parts, but the many parts make up one whole body. So it is with the body of Christ. Some of us are Jews, some are Gentiles, some are slaves, and some are free. But we have all been baptized into one body by one Spirit, and we all share the same Spirit.*

All believers together form God's family, but only by meeting together can you bond. The physical church is a place where Christians learn to work together in unity and where the differences between people are reconciled by the Holy Spirit. When you meet together, you can build one another up and help one another.

REVELATION 19:7-8 | *Let us be glad and rejoice, and let us give honor to [the Lord]. For the time has come for the wedding feast of the Lamb, and his bride has prepared herself. She has been given the finest of pure white linen to wear.*

The church is Christ's bride—a picture of the intimate fellowship that God's people will enjoy with him.

Why should I be involved in church?

PSALM 27:4 | *The one thing I ask of the LORD—the thing I seek most—is to live in the house of the LORD all the days of my life, delighting in the LORD's perfections and meditating in his Temple.*

PSALM 84:4 | *What joy for those who can live in your house, always singing your praises.*

Even though God lives in the heart of every believer, he also lives in the community of the church. When the church is gathered together, it meets God in a special way. Just as actually being at a concert or sports event is so much more exciting than just watching on television, participating with other believers in worship is also more meaningful.

ROMANS 12:4-5 | *Just as our bodies have many parts and each part has a special function, so it is with Christ's body. We are many parts of one body, and we all belong to each other.*

God has given every believer special gifts—some are great organizers and administrators, while others are gifted musicians, teachers, and dishwashers! When everyone in a congregation uses his or her gifts to serve, the church becomes a powerful force for good, a strong witness for Jesus, and a mighty army to combat Satan's attacks against God's people in the community. The church needs you, for the body of Christ is not complete unless you are there!

HEBREWS 10:25 | *Let us not neglect our meeting together, as some people do, but encourage one another, especially now that the day of his return is drawing near.*

Good friends are a wonderful gift, but fellowship at church among other believers is unique because the living God is in your midst. The church brings people together who have a common perspective on life. Christian fellowship provides a place of honest sharing about the things that really matter, encouragement to stay strong in the face of temptation and persecution, and unique wisdom to deal with problems.

COMMITMENT

How do I know what to be committed to?

PROVERBS 3:1-4 | *My child, never forget the things I have taught you. Store my commands in your heart. If you do this, you will live many years, and your life will be satisfying. Never let loyalty and kindness leave you! Tie them around your neck as a reminder. Write them deep within your heart. Then you will find favor with both God and people, and you will earn a good reputation.*

You can fool people for a while by your words and actions, but who you are on the inside will ultimately show itself on the outside. Your words and actions will reflect your heart. For example, committing to worship shows that God comes first in your heart. Committing yourself to kindness shows a commitment to serving others. God promises that when your heart's first commitment is to know and love God, then you will gain a good reputation with others and with God.

COMMUNICATION

How does God communicate with me?

2 TIMOTHY 3:16-17 | *All Scripture is inspired by God and is useful to teach us what is true and to make us realize what is wrong in our lives. It corrects us when we are wrong and teaches us to do what is right. God uses it to prepare and equip his people to do every good work.*

God communicates with you through his Word, the Bible. Read it daily to keep in touch with him.

COLOSSIANS 2:9 | *In Christ lives all the fullness of God in a human body.*

HEBREWS 1:1-2 | *Long ago God spoke many times and in many ways to our ancestors through the prophets. And now in these final days, he has spoken to us through his Son.*

God communicates with you through his Son, Jesus Christ. Talk with him often throughout your day.

JOHN 14:26 | *When the Father sends the Advocate as my representative—that is, the Holy Spirit—he will teach you everything and will remind you of everything I have told you.*

ROMANS 8:16 | *His Spirit joins with our spirit to affirm that we are God's children.*

God communicates with you through his Holy Spirit. Pay special attention to the way he speaks to your heart and spirit.

ROMANS 2:14-15 | *Even Gentiles, who do not have God's written law, show that they know his law when they instinctively obey it, even without having heard it. They demonstrate that God's law is written in their hearts, for their own conscience and thoughts either accuse them or tell them they are doing right.*

God communicates with you through your conscience, which is your God-given, internal radar to help you know right from wrong. Always listen to your conscience. If you neglect it, it will become dull and eventually you will no longer hear it.

PSALM 19:1-4 | *The heavens proclaim the glory of God. The skies display his craftsmanship. Day after day they continue to speak; night after night they make him known. They speak without a sound or word; their voice is never heard. Yet their message has gone throughout the earth, and their words to all the world.*

ROMANS 1:19-20 | *They know the truth about God because he has made it obvious to them. For ever since the world was created, people have seen the earth and sky. Through everything God made, they can clearly see his invisible qualities—his eternal power and divine nature. So they have no excuse for not knowing God.*

God communicates with you through his creation. All nature sings about a majestic God who created rhythm and harmony in the seasons, babbling brooks, and crashing ocean waves. Nature shouts the power of God in the starry heavens, the roar of thunder, earthquakes, hurricanes, and glorious snowcapped mountains. But nature also whispers about God's mind-boggling attention to detail in the wings of a butterfly, the bark of a tree, the variety of plants, and the complexity of a strand of DNA. Look for God's fingerprints, footprints, and even voiceprints in his handiwork, and you will not be able to miss him.

JOHN 11:25, 43-44 | *Jesus [said], "I am the resurrection and the life. Anyone who believes in me will live, even after dying." . . . Then Jesus shouted, "Lazarus, come out!" And the dead man came out, his hands and feet bound in graveclothes, his face wrapped in a headcloth. Jesus told them, "Unwrap him and let him go!"*

ACTS 14:16-17 | *In the past [God] permitted all the nations to go their own ways, but he never left them without evidence of himself and his goodness. For instance, he sends you rain and good crops and gives you food and joyful hearts.*

God communicates through the miraculous. There are great miracles told about in the Bible, such as the resurrection of the dead and everyday miracles like a baby's birth. As you begin to recognize the miracles of God all around you, you will recognize the marvelous ways he speaks to you.

1 SAMUEL 3:7-10 | *Samuel did not yet know the LORD because he had never had a message from the LORD before. So the LORD called a third time, and once more Samuel got up and went to Eli. "Here I am. Did you call me?" Then Eli realized it was the LORD who was calling the boy. So he said to Samuel, "Go and lie down again, and if someone calls again, say, 'Speak, LORD, your servant is listening.'" So Samuel went back to bed. And the LORD came and called as before, "Samuel! Samuel!" And Samuel replied, "Speak, your servant is listening."*

ISAIAH 45:2, 4 | *This is what the LORD says: "I will go before you, Cyrus. . . . And why have I called you for this work? Why did I call you by name when you did not know me? It is for the sake of Jacob my servant, Israel my chosen one."*

God communicates with you through other people. Most of the time he uses godly people to give you spiritual advice and help you mature in your faith. But sometimes he uses people who don't know him to unwittingly communicate his truth to you.

How can I know God is speaking to me?

HEBREWS 4:12 | *The word of God is alive and powerful. It is sharper than the sharpest two-edged sword, cutting between soul and spirit, between joint and marrow. It exposes our innermost thoughts and desires.*

Just as a piano is tuned against a standard tuning fork, so you become in tune with God only when you compare yourself against his standards for living found in the Bible. As God communicates to you through the Bible, you will begin to "hear" or discern just what he wants of you. As your "spiritual hearing" is tuned, you will be able to hear more clearly when God calls you to a certain task that he has reserved just for you. Would God say you are a good listener?

PSALM 46:10 | *Be still, and know that I am God! I will be honored by every nation. I will be honored throughout the world.*

MARK 1:35 | *Before daybreak the next morning, Jesus got up and went out to an isolated place to pray.*

Prayer is talking to God and building a relationship with him. Good conversation also includes listening— allowing God to speak to you. Only when you hear God can he make his wisdom and resources available to you. Sometimes you must spend time in his presence without feeling the need to verbalize prayer. Just begin to think about God and listen, ready to hear him speak to your heart and mind. As you meditate, you will learn to recognize the distinction between your own ideas and the prompting of an idea from him.

1 CORINTHIANS 2:16 | *"Who can know the LORD's thoughts? Who knows enough to teach him?" But we understand these things, for we have the mind of Christ.*

When you become a Christian, the Holy Spirit helps you understand the mind of Christ. He gives you guidance, wisdom, and discernment that are not available to those who don't love the Lord.

COMMUNITY

Why is it important to meet together as a community of believers?

1 CORINTHIANS 5:4 I *You must call a meeting of the church. I will be present with you in spirit, and so will the power of our Lord Jesus.*

EPHESIANS 4:16 I *[Christ] makes the whole body fit together perfectly. As each part does its own special work, it helps the other parts grow, so that the whole body is healthy and growing and full of love.*

We were created for community. Jesus commissioned the church to be a body of believers, not a collection of individuals. Being connected to other people in loving relationships is important to a life filled with hope. Living in isolation makes us vulnerable to discouragement and despair. When we are connected to a community of believers, we have a place to worship together, to support one another, and to have fellowship that can keep us steady on God's path even during the most difficult times. Because Jesus promises to be with us, when we gather as a body of believers we can experience God's presence in a unique and powerful way.

COMPROMISE

How do I live in today's culture without compromising my convictions?

DANIEL 1:8, 12, 14 | *Daniel was determined not to defile himself by eating the food . . . given . . . by the king. He asked . . . permission not to eat these unacceptable foods. . . . "Please test us for ten days on a diet of vegetables and water," Daniel said. . . . The attendant agreed to Daniel's suggestion.*

Never be afraid to take a stand for what you know is right and true, but do so in a respectful, humble manner. You will be surprised how often you will be admired for sticking to your beliefs, even if others disagree with them. But even if you meet resistance, you must not compromise by going against God's Word.

EXODUS 34:12 | *Be very careful never to make a treaty with the people who live in the land where you are going. If you do, you will follow their evil ways and be trapped.*

REVELATION 2:14 | *[God said,] "I have a few complaints against you. You tolerate some among you whose teaching is like that of Balaam, who showed Balak how to trip up the people of Israel. He taught them to sin."*

Don't allow compromise to dull your sensitivity to sin. A "little" sin now and then can lead to a life defined by sin.

JUDGES 16:15-17 | *Delilah pouted, "How can you tell me, 'I love you,' when you don't share your secrets with me?". . . She tormented him with her nagging day after day until . . . Samson shared his secret with her.*

You are most likely to compromise in areas where you are spiritually weak. Learn to recognize where you are vulnerable so that you are prepared when the temptation to compromise comes.

CONDEMNATION

Will God condemn me for my sins?

ISAIAH 26:21 | *The LORD is coming from heaven to punish the people of the earth for their sins.*

ROMANS 2:5-6 | *Because you are stubborn and refuse to turn from your sin, you are storing up terrible punishment for yourself. For a day of anger is coming, when God's righteous judgment will be revealed. He will judge everyone according to what they have done.*

Not only did God create truth, he *is* truth itself, and therefore sets the standard for truth and justice. Judgment and punishment are promised for all sin.

ROMANS 3:25 | *God presented Jesus as the sacrifice for sin. People are made right with God when they believe that Jesus sacrificed his life, shedding his blood.*

COLOSSIANS 1:22 | *[God] has reconciled you to himself through the death of Christ in his physical body. As a result, he has brought you into his own presence, and you are holy and blameless as you stand before him without a single fault.*

If you have put your faith in Jesus, and so belong to him, you have been freed forever from condemnation. You will not be condemned, because you recognize and accept that

Jesus bore the ultimate punishment for your sins—death—when he died in your place. He declares you "Not guilty."

CONFESSION

Why is confession so essential to my relationship with God?

PSALM 32:5 | *Finally, I confessed all my sins to you and stopped trying to hide my guilt. I said to myself, "I will confess my rebellion to the LORD." And you forgave me! All my guilt is gone.*

MATTHEW 10:32 | *[Jesus said,] "Everyone who acknowledges me publicly here on earth, I will also acknowledge before my Father in heaven."*

ROMANS 10:9 | *If you confess with your mouth that Jesus is Lord and believe in your heart that God raised him from the dead, you will be saved.*

JAMES 5:16 | *Confess your sins to each other and pray for each other so that you may be healed. The earnest prayer of a righteous person has great power and produces wonderful results.*

1 JOHN 1:9 | *If we confess our sins to him, he is faithful and just to forgive us.*

Confession is the acknowledgment of guilt to other people or to God. When you acknowledge the ugliness of sin, you find it embarrassing and sometimes painful. Perhaps the embarrassment is in letting others see deeply into your life, of being vulnerable to ridicule. But confession is a necessary part of knowing God, being released from guilt through his forgiveness, and finding new beginnings. Confession is essential to knowing God because it is only through the humility of admitting wrong that you can establish honesty and trust with him. Confession is essential to being freed from the eternal consequences of sin because it brings about God's forgiveness. And confessing your allegiance to God is essential to giving you the courage to stand up for your faith when it is tested. It is only through confession that you maintain an open line of communication with God, putting yourself in the position to experience a deep and real relationship with him.

What happens when I confess my sin?

PSALM 103:3, 10-12 | *He forgives all my sins and heals all my diseases. . . . He does not punish us for all our sins; he does not deal harshly with us, as we deserve. For his unfailing love toward those who fear him is as great as the height of the heavens above the earth. He has removed our sins as far from us as the east is from the west.*

ISAIAH 43:25 | *[The Lord said,] "I—yes, I alone—will blot out your sins for my own sake and will never think of them again."*

COLOSSIANS 1:22 | *[God] has reconciled you to himself through the death of Christ. . . . As a result, he has brought you into his own presence, and you are holy and blameless as you stand before him without a single fault.*

When you confess your sins and trust Jesus Christ, your sins are wiped away. They will not be held against you—God actually forgets about them. You are freely and fully pardoned by the Lord and should forgive yourself as well.

CONFLICT

Why do I still have this inner conflict, wanting to please God but knowing I often don't?

PROVERBS 28:14 | *Blessed are those who fear to do wrong, but the stubborn are headed for serious trouble.*

Most of us struggle with inner conflict. We have given our lives to follow Christ, but the old human nature still exists. We don't want to do wrong, but we so often do (see Romans 7:14-25). We know the attitudes and behavior that Christ desires, but we also know how hard it is to live that way all the time. Ironically this kind of conflict is a good thing because it shows that your conscience is still sensitive to sin and that you truly desire to do what is right. It is that attitude that causes God to call you blessed.

CONNECTED TO GOD

What happens when I stay close to Jesus?

JOHN 15:4-5 | *[Jesus said,] "Remain in me, and I will remain in you. For a branch cannot produce fruit if it is severed from the vine, and you cannot be fruitful unless you remain in me. Yes, I am the vine; you are the branches. Those who remain in me, and I in them, will produce much fruit. For apart from me you can do nothing."*

When you are connected to Jesus, he turns your simple acts into something profound and purposeful. For example, he turns your simple act of singing into a profound chorus of praise that ministers to an entire congregation. He turns your simple act of telling others your faith story into profound moments in the hearts of friends who suddenly realize their own need for salvation. Stay connected to Jesus and let him turn your simple acts of service into profound works for the Kingdom of God.

CONSCIENCE

How does my conscience work?

PROVERBS 2:1, 9 I *My child, listen to what I say. . . . Then you will understand what is right, just, and fair, and you will find the right way to go.*

ROMANS 1:19-20 I *They know the truth about God because he has made it obvious to them. For ever since the world was created, people have seen the earth and sky. Through everything God made, they can clearly see his invisible qualities—his eternal power and divine nature. So they have no excuse for not knowing God.*

ROMANS 1:21 I *Yes, they knew God, but they wouldn't worship him as God or even give him thanks. And they began to think up foolish ideas of what God was like. As a result, their minds became dark and confused.*

Conscience is the innate part of you that helps you tell whether you are in line with God's will. Your conscience is God's gift to you to keep you sensitive to his moral code. But you must use the gift. If you don't listen to and obey your conscience, it will become dull and you will have difficulty hearing it. In addition, it will malfunction if not properly cared for. Your conscience will function effectively only when you stay close to God, spend time in his Word, and make an effort to understand yourself and your own personal tendencies toward sin. If your conscience is working faithfully, it will activate your heart and mind to know what is right from wrong. You will have a strong inner sense, a voice of accountability, to do what is right. If you have a reputation for not always doing the right thing or if you find yourself unmoved by evil, it may be an indication that your conscience has become dull or inactive. Let God, through his holy Word, sharpen and resensitize your conscience. Then it will speak to you in concert with God himself.

What happens when I ignore my conscience?

1 TIMOTHY 1:19 | *Cling to your faith in Christ, and keep your conscience clear. For some people have deliberately violated their consciences; as a result, their faith has been shipwrecked.*

God warns that if you consistently ignore your conscience, your faith will be shipwrecked. When you sin, you are deliberately going against your conscience. You know what you are doing is wrong because your conscience tells you so, but you do it anyway because it is so appealing. When you consistently go against what your conscience tells you, you can train yourself to not hear it calling out to you, warning you of danger. Without a strong conscience, you become insensitive to sin and hard hearted. In a sense you have "tricked" it into thinking all is well when all is really not well. Have you been listening to your conscience lately? The answer to that question will tell you if you are growing in your faith or neglecting it.

CONTROL

If I shouldn't let anything control me, why should I submit to God's control?

ROMANS 8:6, 9 | *Letting your sinful nature control your mind leads to death. But letting the Spirit control your mind leads to life and peace. . . . But you are not controlled by your sinful nature. You are controlled by the Spirit if you have the Spirit of God living in you.*

GALATIANS 5:22-23, 25 | *The Holy Spirit produces this kind of fruit in our lives: love, joy, peace, patience, kindness, goodness, faithfulness, gentleness, and self-control. . . . Let us follow the Spirit's leading in every part of our lives.*

God's control, through the work of his Holy Spirit, is the only kind of control that produces completely positive results.

ROMANS 6:14, 18 | *Sin is no longer your master, for you no longer live under the requirements of the law. Instead, you live under the freedom of God's grace. . . . Now you are free from your slavery to sin, and you have become slaves to righteous living.*

2 CORINTHIANS 5:17 | *Anyone who belongs to Christ has become a new person. The old life is gone; a new life has begun!*

Submission to God frees you to live a new life, one with purpose and fulfillment.

ROMANS 6:16, 22 | *Don't you realize that you become the slave of whatever you choose to obey? You can be a slave to sin, which leads to death, or you can choose to obey God, which leads to righteous living. . . . But now you are free from the power of sin and have become slaves of God. Now you do those things that lead to holiness and result in eternal life.*

GALATIANS 6:8 | *Those who live only to satisfy their own sinful nature will harvest decay and death from that sinful nature. But those who live to please the Spirit will harvest everlasting life from the Spirit.*

Submission to God results in freedom from the power of sin and in eternal life.

CONVICTIONS

How do convictions strengthen my life of faith?

DANIEL 1:8 | *Daniel was determined not to defile himself by eating the food and wine given to [him] by the king. He asked the chief of staff for permission not to eat these unacceptable foods.*

EPHESIANS 4:13-15 | *[Equipping God's people] will continue until we all come to such unity in our faith and knowledge of God's Son that we will be mature in the Lord, measuring up to the full and complete standard of Christ. Then we will no longer be immature like children. We won't be tossed and blown about by every wind of new teaching. We will not be influenced when people try to trick us with lies so clever they sound like the truth. Instead, we will speak the truth in love, growing in every way more and more like Christ, who is the head of his body, the church.*

Conviction is more than just a belief; it is a commitment to a belief. What you think, say, and do shows the level of your conviction. For example, when you believe Jesus Christ is who he claims to be, then out of this belief should come the conviction to live by his teachings. Convictions prepare you to effectively live a life of faith and to defend your faith when necessary. Convictions hold you steady on the path of life and help you to faithfully live and act out your belief in God in practical ways. Keep your convictions firm and your life will be a great story of faith.

In a different sense, conviction can also refer to the work of the Holy Spirit in your heart, telling you what is right and wrong. Without the Holy Spirit's convicting your heart, you would be unprepared to face temptation and would easily give in.

What are some basic convictions I must have to live out my faith effectively?

HEBREWS 6:18 | *God has given both his promise and his oath. These two things are unchangeable because it is impossible for God to lie. Therefore, we who have fled to him for refuge can have great confidence as we hold to the hope that lies before us.*

Be confident that God always keeps his promises.

EXODUS 20:1-3 | *God gave the people all these instructions: "I am the LORD your God, who rescued you. . . . You must not have any other god but me."*

Accept that God must have first priority in your life.

HEBREWS 11:1 | *Faith is the confidence that what we hope for will actually happen; it gives us assurance about things we cannot see.*

Be assured that your faith in God is valid. You can't see God, but you can see the evidence of God as he does his supernatural work through people. This gives you a confident hope that one day you will see what you can't now.

COLOSSIANS 1:23 | *You must continue to believe this truth and stand firmly in it. Don't drift away from the assurance you received when you heard the Good News.*

2 TIMOTHY 3:16 | *All Scripture is inspired by God and is useful to teach us what is true and to make us realize what is wrong in our lives. It corrects us when we are wrong and teaches us to do what is right.*

Believe that the Bible was written by God and is God's truth for all matters of faith and life.

JOHN 3:16 | *God loved the world so much that he gave his one and only Son, so that everyone who believes in him will not perish but have eternal life.*

ACTS 2:37-39 | *Peter's words pierced their hearts, and they said to him and to the other apostles, "Brothers, what should we do?" Peter replied, "Each of you must repent of your sins and turn to God, and be baptized in the name of Jesus Christ for the forgiveness of your sins. Then you will receive the gift of the Holy Spirit. This promise is to you."*

ROMANS 10:9 | *If you confess with your mouth that Jesus is Lord and believe in your heart that God raised him from the dead, you will be saved.*

2 CORINTHIANS 5:17 | *Anyone who belongs to Christ has become a new person. The old life is gone; a new life has begun!*

1 JOHN 1:9 | *If we confess our sins to him, he is faithful and just to forgive us our sins and to cleanse us.*

Accept that salvation is of God. If you are truly sorry for your sins and confess them to God (repentance) and if you believe that God's Son, Jesus, died for you, taking upon himself the punishment you deserve for your sins, then God forgives you and gives you the gift of salvation. The moment this happens, the Holy Spirit enters your life and begins transforming you into a new person on the inside. Then you know that your life can and will be different.

EPHESIANS 4:15 | *We will speak the truth in love, growing in every way more and more like Christ, who is the head of his body, the church.*

Be confident that if you live by the truths in God's Word, you will become more and more like Jesus, which is your primary goal.

ROMANS 8:38-39 | *Nothing can ever separate us from God's love. Neither death nor life, neither angels nor demons, neither our fears for today nor our worries about tomorrow—not even the powers of hell can separate us from God's love. No power in the sky above or in the earth below—indeed, nothing in all creation will ever be able to separate us from the love of God that is revealed in Christ Jesus our Lord.*

Know that nothing can separate you from God's love for you.

JEREMIAH 17:7 | *Blessed are those who trust in the LORD and have made the LORD their hope and confidence.*

HEBREWS 10:35 | *Do not throw away this confident trust in the Lord. Remember the great reward it brings you!*

Trust the Lord to bring you great blessings and eternal rewards.

PSALM 17:6 | *I am praying to you because I know you will answer, O God. Bend down and listen as I pray.*

Believe that God answers prayer.

PSALM 16:8 | *I know the LORD is always with me. I will not be shaken, for he is right beside me.*

Have faith that God is always with you.

JOB 42:1-2 | *Job [said] to the LORD: "I know that you can do anything, and no one can stop you."*

PSALM 135:5 | *I know the greatness of the LORD—that our Lord is greater than any other god.*

Rest in the knowledge that no one is greater than God. He is sovereign and all-powerful.

DEATH

Why is death so scary?

JOHN 11:25-26 | *Jesus [said], "I am the resurrection and the life. Anyone who believes in me will live, even after dying. Everyone who lives in me and believes in me will never ever die."*

Why are we so afraid to die? Why do we try so hard to keep living? Because we are uncertain of what happens after that. On this side of death, we at least know the rules of how things work, even if we don't like everything that happens. To die physically is to leave our earthly bodies and our places in the earthly community. To die spiritually is to miss eternal residence in heaven with God and his people and to be separated from God forever. When Christians die physically, we become even more alive as we take up residence in heaven. For those of us who believe Jesus is our Savior, death is not the end, but only the beginning of an eternity of unspeakable joy with the Lord and with other believers.

What will my body be like after I die and am resurrected?

1 CORINTHIANS 15:35, 53 | *Someone may ask, "How will the dead be raised? What kind of bodies will they have?" . . . Our dying bodies must be transformed into bodies that will never die; our mortal bodies must be transformed into immortal bodies.*

1 CORINTHIANS 15:43-44 | *Our bodies are buried in brokenness, but they will be raised in glory. They are buried in weakness, but they will be raised in strength. They are buried as natural human bodies, but they will be raised as spiritual bodies. For just as there are natural bodies, there are also spiritual bodies.*

Your resurrected body will be a physical body, as you have now, but it will also have many supernatural characteristics. For example, you may be able to walk through walls as Jesus did with his resurrected body (see John 20:19, 26). Most importantly, your new body won't decay from the effects of sin. You will never be sick or in pain again, nor will your mind think sinful thoughts (see Revelation 21:4). You will be fully and finally perfect.

DECISIONS

Does each decision I make really matter that much?

PSALM 17:5 | *My steps have stayed on your path; I have not wavered from following you.*

PROVERBS 3:6 | *Seek his will in all you do, and he will show you which path to take.*

PROVERBS 16:3 | *Commit your actions to the LORD, and your plans will succeed.*

HOSEA 6:3 | *Oh, that we might know the LORD! Let us press on to know him. He will respond to us as surely as the arrival of dawn or the coming of rains in early spring.*

Making right decisions is like hiking; each step puts you a little farther ahead on the path. Sometimes the right decision is simply being faithful in little things. God's will for you today is to obey him, serve others, read his Word, and do what is right. If you stay in the center of his will today and every day, you can be sure that you will be in the center of his will twenty years from now. When you have been faithful over time, there comes a point at which you are close enough to God to recognize his leading in your life.

Should I "put out a fleece"?

JUDGES 6:39 | *Gideon said to God, . . . "Let me use the fleece for one more test. This time let the fleece remain dry while the ground around it is wet with dew."*

"Putting out a fleece" is a phrase that comes from the story of Gideon found in the Bible. It means that you designate a sign that will confirm you made the right decision and then ask God to make that sign occur. Great caution must be exercised when putting out a fleece because it tends to limit the options of a God who has unlimited options available to you. It is also dangerous because it can be used to blame God if the decision doesn't go the way you wanted. Don't try to force God to make a decision from your limited range of options. Let God decide, from his unlimited options, how best to lead you.

DESIRES

How do desires affect me?

PSALM 42:1-2 | *As the deer longs for streams of water, so I long for you, O God. I thirst for God, the living God. When can I go and stand before him?*

PSALM 73:25 | *Whom have I in heaven but you? I desire you more than anything on earth.*

ISAIAH 26:8-9 | *LORD, we show our trust in you by obeying your laws; our heart's desire is to glorify your name. All night long I search for you; in the morning I earnestly seek for God.*

ROMANS 13:14 | *Clothe yourself with the presence of the Lord Jesus Christ. And don't let yourself think about ways to indulge your evil desires.*

PHILIPPIANS 2:13 | *God is working in you, giving you the desire and the power to do what pleases him.*

You are motivated by what you really want. A golfer may strive for the perfect drive, an artist for rave reviews, a business executive for higher profit margins, a student for straight A's. An examination of the things you really desire reveals the passion and priorities of your heart. Your chances of accomplishing your goals increase in proportion to the intensity of your commitment. Remarkably, the Bible indicates it is possible for human beings to know and experience the God of the universe in a personal way. What more lofty goal could you aspire to? God desires an intimate and transforming relationship with his people. To experience him, you must pursue him with all your heart. The Bible consistently encourages you to ask, "Is God just one among many pursuits, or is God chief of all my desires?" If your friends were to determine what you want more than anything, would they say the desire of your heart is a relationship with God? What would others guess is your most driving goal? When you desire God more than anything, your chances of accomplishing great things through his power increase as you intensify your commitment to him.

Why do some Bible passages say desire is a good thing and other passages say it's not?

GALATIANS 5:16-17 | *Let the Holy Spirit guide your lives. Then you won't be doing what your sinful nature craves. The sinful nature wants to do evil, which is just the opposite of what the Spirit wants. And the Spirit gives us desires that are the opposite of what the sinful nature desires. These two forces are constantly fighting each other.*

PHILIPPIANS 2:13 | *God is working in you, giving you the desire and the power to do what pleases him.*

JAMES 1:14-15 | *Temptation comes from our own desires, which entice us and drag us away. These desires give birth to sinful actions. And when sin is allowed to grow, it gives birth to death.*

God created desire within you as a means of expressing yourself. Desire is good and healthy if directed toward the proper object: that which is good and right and God-honoring. It is ironic that a desire can be right or wrong, depending upon your motive and the object of your desire. For example, the desire to love someone of the opposite sex, if directed to your spouse, is healthy and right. But that same desire directed to someone who is not your spouse is adultery. The desire to lead an organization is healthy if your motive is to serve others, but unhealthy and wrong if your motive is to have the power to control them.

DIGNITY

How does following God give me dignity?

GENESIS 1:27 | *God created human beings in his own image. In the image of God he created them; male and female he created them.*

PSALM 8:5 | *[The Lord] made [human beings] only a little lower than God and crowned them with glory and honor.*

PSALM 149:4-5 | *The LORD delights in his people; he crowns the humble with victory. Let the faithful rejoice that he honors them.*

Dignity is the quality of worth and significance that every human being has been given because we were all created in the image of God. Dignity has two sides—recognizing one's own worth before God and recognizing that same worth in others. Unfortunately, it is human nature to rank everyone from important to insignificant. A proper view of dignity motivates you to see others as God sees them: worthy of your love and respect no matter where they live or what they do. This fosters a deep respect for others as you build them up rather than devaluing them. On the other side of dignity, when you behave respectably, have self-control and strong faith, and are loving and patient, you show personal dignity. Furthermore, when you realize how esteemed you are by God, the opinions of others matter less.

DISAPPOINTMENT

What disappoints God?

GENESIS 6:5-6 | *The LORD observed the extent of human wickedness on the earth, and he saw that everything they thought or imagined was consistently and totally evil. So the LORD was sorry he had ever made them and put them on the earth. It broke his heart.*

Wickedness and evil of any kind disappoint God.

HEBREWS 3:17-18 | *Who made God angry for forty years? Wasn't it the people who sinned, whose corpses lay in the wilderness? And to whom was God speaking when he took an oath that they would never enter his rest? Wasn't it the people who disobeyed him?*

Sin and disobedience disappoint God.

MALACHI 1:8, 10 | *"When you give blind animals as sacrifices, isn't that wrong? And isn't it wrong to offer animals that are crippled and diseased? . . . I am not pleased with you," says the LORD of Heaven's Armies, "and I will not accept your offerings."*

Giving God less than your best disappoints him.

2 TIMOTHY 2:4 | *Soldiers don't get tied up in the affairs of civilian life, for then they cannot please the officer who enlisted them.*

Letting other things in your life overshadow the Lord disappoints him.

What should I do if I feel God has disappointed me?

EXODUS 5:22 | *Moses went back to the LORD and protested.*

Talk it through with him.

JOHN 11:21 | *Martha said to Jesus, "Lord, if only you had been here, my brother would not have died."*

Be honest with him about your thoughts and feelings. He knows them anyway, so why try to hide them?

2 CORINTHIANS 12:8-10 | *Three different times I begged the Lord to take [the thorn in my flesh] away. Each time he said, "My grace is all you need. My power works best in weakness." So now I am glad to boast about my weaknesses, so that the power of Christ can work through me. That's why I take pleasure in my weaknesses, and in the insults, hardships, persecutions, and troubles that I suffer for Christ. For when I am weak, then I am strong.*

Wrestle with the question of why God won't just take away your pain. Ask him what work he has decided to do because of your weakness. It is through this struggle that you discover your purpose in life.

Is there a way to avoid or minimize disappointment in my life?

HAGGAI 1:6, 9 | *You have planted much but harvest little. . . . Why? Because my house lies in ruins, says the LORD of Heaven's Armies, while all of you are busy building your own fine houses.*

Put God first. Give him the best minutes of your day, the first part of your money, the highest priority in your life. By doing this, you will discover the rewards and satisfaction of a relationship with the God who created you and loves you.

PSALM 22:5 | *They cried out to you and were saved. They trusted in you and were never disgraced.*

PSALM 34:2 | *I will boast only in the LORD; let all who are helpless take heart.*

1 PETER 2:6 | *As the Scriptures say, "I am placing a cornerstone in Jerusalem, chosen for great honor, and anyone who trusts in him will never be disgraced."*

If you live by the principles of Scripture given by God himself, you will face less disappointment because you will have fewer consequences resulting from sinful actions.

GALATIANS 6:4 | *Pay careful attention to your own work, for then you will get the satisfaction of a job well done, and you won't need to compare yourself to anyone else.*

The satisfaction of doing right and performing a job well will minimize disappointment.

How should I respond to disappointment?

GALATIANS 6:9 | *Let's not get tired of doing what is good. At just the right time we will reap a harvest of blessing if we don't give up.*

When others don't seem to notice or appreciate your good deeds or when you don't see them making a difference, you can be disappointed. But anything good you do has immense value, both for you and for others. Don't let disappointment keep you from doing good, if for no other reason than to enjoy the blessings God will reward you with when you meet him face-to-face.

ECCLESIASTES 10:8-9 | *When you dig a well, you might fall in. When you demolish an old wall, you could be bitten by a snake. When you work in a quarry, stones might fall and crush you. When you chop wood, there is danger with each stroke of your ax.*

To live the great adventure of life, you must accept the risks that come with the adventure. See your disappointments as stepping-stones to something greater ahead.

DISCERNMENT

What happens when I use discernment?

PSALM 119:34 | *Give me understanding and I will obey your instructions; I will put them into practice with all my heart.*

PROVERBS 2:1-6 | *My child, listen to what I say, and treasure my commands. Tune your ears to wisdom, and concentrate on*

*understanding. Cry out for insight, and ask for understanding.
Search for them as you would for silver; seek them like hidden
treasures. Then you will understand what it means to fear the
LORD, and you will gain knowledge of God. For the LORD grants
wisdom! From his mouth come knowledge and understanding.*

PHILIPPIANS 1:10 | *I want you to understand what really matters,
so that you may live pure and blameless lives until the day of
Christ's return.*

HEBREWS 5:12-14 | *You need someone to teach you again the basic
things about God's word. You are like babies who need milk
and cannot eat solid food. For someone who lives on milk is still
an infant and doesn't know how to do what is right. Solid food
is for those who are mature, who through training have the skill
to recognize the difference between right and wrong.*

Discernment is the process of training yourself to distinguish
between right and wrong by disciplining your conscience,
mind, senses, and body. The Bible says that discernment is
necessary to mature in your faith. It also says that recognizing the difference between right and wrong is a developed
skill. When you grow and mature in your faith, you are able
to recognize temptation before it has engulfed you. You can
also learn to recognize truth from falsehood and God's voice
from other voices. Knowing the Scriptures helps you discern
false teaching when someone is using a passage of Scripture
incorrectly. When you practice discernment and train yourself to detect right from wrong, you can avoid the pitfalls and
confusion so many people fall into. Life works better and you
live better because you are following God's intended path
for you.

DOUBT

When I'm struggling in life and have doubts about God, does it mean I am lacking faith?

GENESIS 15:8 | *Abram [said], "O Sovereign LORD, how can I be sure . . . ?"*

MATTHEW 11:2-3 | *John the Baptist . . . sent his disciples to ask Jesus, "Are you the Messiah we've been expecting, or should we keep looking for someone else?"*

JOHN 20:29 | *Jesus [said], "You believe because you have seen me. Blessed are those who believe without seeing me."*

HEBREWS 13:5 | *God has said, "I will never fail you. I will never abandon you."*

Many people in the Bible who are considered to be "pillars of faith" had moments of doubt. This doesn't mean that they didn't trust in God but rather that their faith was being challenged in a new way. When you have moments of doubt, you are probably in new territory. Don't let your doubt drive you away from God. Instead, use your doubt as a moment to begin a new conversation with God. He welcomes your doubts as an opportunity to give you new insights about his love for you and how you can better relate to him. As your doubts cause you to reach for him, you will find he is always there.

What if I find it hard to believe that there was a literal historical person named Jesus and that he really rose from the dead?

PSALM 22:16 | *My enemies . . . have pierced my hands and feet.*

DANIEL 9:24-25 | *A period of seventy sets of seven has been decreed for your people and your holy city to finish their rebellion, to put an end to their sin, to atone for their guilt, to bring in everlasting righteousness, to confirm the prophetic vision, and to anoint the Most Holy Place. Now listen and understand! Seven sets of seven plus sixty-two sets of seven will pass from the time the command is given to rebuild Jerusalem until a ruler—the Anointed One—comes.*

MICAH 5:2, 4-5 | *You, O Bethlehem Ephrathah, are only a small village among all the people of Judah. Yet a ruler of Israel will come from you, one whose origins are from the distant past. . . . And he will stand to lead his flock with the LORD's strength, in the majesty of the name of the LORD his God. . . . And he will be the source of peace.*

More than four dozen predictions were made from prophets in the Old Testament regarding Jesus. These predictions, or prophecies, were so specific about one person that they would be virtually impossible for humans to fulfill, even if people had tried to. Yet evidence is overwhelming that Jesus fulfilled all of them.

ISAIAH 53:8 | *Unjustly condemned, he was led away. No one cared that he died without descendants, that his life was cut short in midstream. But he was struck down for the rebellion of my people.*

1 CORINTHIANS 15:3-8 | *I passed on to you what was most important and what had also been passed on to me. Christ died for our sins, just as the Scriptures said. He was buried, and he was raised from the dead on the third day, just as the Scriptures said. He was seen by Peter and then by the Twelve. After that, he was seen by more*

than 500 of his followers at one time, . . . Then he was seen by James and later by all the apostles. Last of all, . . . I also saw him.

1 JOHN 1:1-3 | *We proclaim to you the one who existed from the beginning, whom we have heard and seen. We saw him with our own eyes and touched him with our own hands. He is the Word of life. This one who is life itself was revealed to us, and we have seen him. And now we testify and proclaim to you that he is the one who is eternal life. He was with the Father, and then he was revealed to us. We proclaim to you what we ourselves have actually seen and heard so that you may have fellowship with us.*

The resurrected Jesus Christ was predicted by countless prophets and seen by countless witnesses. Upon seeing Jesus resurrected, the disciples were transformed from cowards into courageous witnesses who could not be silenced. Most of them died for what they believed in, which is something no one would do for a lie.

How can my faith be strengthened during times of doubting God?

JUDGES 7:2-4 | *The LORD said to Gideon, "You have too many warriors with you. If I let all of you fight the Midianites, the Israelites will boast to me that they saved themselves by their own strength. Therefore, tell the people, 'Whoever is timid or afraid may leave this mountain and go home.'" So 22,000 of them went home, leaving only 10,000 who were willing to fight. But the LORD told Gideon, "There are still too many! Bring them down to the spring, and I will test them to determine who will go with you and who will not."*

PSALM 94:19 | *When doubts filled my mind, your comfort gave me renewed hope and cheer.*

Doubt can be a trapdoor to fear, or it can be a doorway to stronger faith. When you doubt God's ability to help you in the face of great odds, but you trust him and he acts, your faith is strengthened. God wants you to express your faith in him *before* he acts. So when God calls you to a task, as he did with Gideon, don't be surprised if at first it seems the obstacles are stacking up against you. This may be a test of your faith; God may be preparing to deepen your faith and character so that you know it is really God who is coming to your rescue, rather than your own efforts. As Gideon's army dwindled, he realized he was no longer in charge—only God could help him now. When you are humble enough to realize that you can't accomplish the job on your own, when you are ready to give God the credit rather than yourself, when you courageously hold on to your belief that God has called you to do something for him, then you are in position to see God at work.

EFFECTIVENESS

I feel like I'm not doing enough for God where I am. Should I move on?

ROMANS 7:4 | *You died to the power of the law when you died with Christ. And now you are united with the one who was raised from the dead. As a result, we can produce a harvest of good deeds for God.*

God wastes nothing but instead uses everything to further his good purposes. He will use you in whatever situation you find yourself. If it feels as if your current role isn't significant, remember that God is preparing you for later service. Make the most of where God has put you right now because serving God right where you are can be holy preparation for where God wants to eventually move you.

ENEMIES

What does it mean to love my enemies?

MATTHEW 5:43-44 | *[Jesus said,] "You have heard the law that says, 'Love your neighbor' and hate your enemy. But I say, love your enemies! Pray for those who persecute you!"*

ROMANS 12:20-21 | *"If your enemies are hungry, feed them. If they are thirsty, give them something to drink. In doing this, you will heap burning coals of shame on their heads." Don't let evil conquer you, but conquer evil by doing good.*

1 PETER 3:9 | *Don't repay evil for evil. Don't retaliate with insults when people insult you. Instead, pay them back with a blessing. That is what God has called you to do, and he will bless you for it.*

Loving your enemies seems unreasonable—unless you realize that you were an enemy of God until he forgave you. When you love your enemies, you see them as Christ does—people in need of grace. Getting to that point takes prayer. You can't pray for others and not feel compassion for them. This is how you can refrain from retaliating when people hurt you, and this is how God can turn enemies into friends.

MATTHEW 18:21-22 | *Peter came to [Jesus] and asked, "Lord, how often should I forgive someone who sins against me? Seven times?" "No, not seven times," Jesus replied, "but seventy times seven!"*

LUKE 6:27-29 | *Love your enemies! Do good to those who hate you. Bless those who curse you. Pray for those who hurt you. If someone slaps you on one cheek, offer the other cheek also. If someone demands your coat, offer your shirt also.*

LUKE 23:34 | *Jesus said, "Father, forgive them, for they don't know what they are doing."*

Respond to your enemies—no matter what they try to do—with forgiveness. Your actions toward your enemies should include prayer for them as well as acts of kindness. Your words should be gentle. Your attitude should not be one of revenge or ill will. This is what sets you apart from the rest of the world, for Jesus did the same.

ISAIAH 53:7 | *He was oppressed and treated harshly, yet he never said a word.*

1 PETER 3:9 | *Don't repay evil for evil.*

At times, your best response to opposition is no response at all. If you repay evil with evil, you stoop to fighting on someone else's terms and you cut yourself off from seeing God's righteous power at work on your behalf.

Are there really spiritual enemies—powers of darkness—trying to attack me?

DANIEL 10:12-13 | *[The man in the vision] said, "Don't be afraid, Daniel. Since the first day you began to pray for understanding and to humble yourself before your God, your request has been heard in heaven. I have come in answer to your prayer. But for twenty-one days the spirit prince of the kingdom of Persia blocked my way. Then Michael, one of the archangels, came to help me."*

MATTHEW 4:1 | *Jesus was led by the Spirit into the wilderness to be tempted there by the devil.*

The Bible clearly teaches that human beings are involved in a spiritual battle. Far from excluding you from this spiritual battle, faith puts you right in the middle of it. You must recognize that you are in a battle for your very soul and arm yourself with weapons that can resist spiritual attacks or you will be defeated (see Ephesians 6:11-18).

EPHESIANS 6:12 | *We are not fighting against flesh-and-blood enemies, but against evil rulers and authorities of the unseen world, against mighty powers in this dark world, and against evil spirits in the heavenly places.*

1 JOHN 2:16 | *The world offers only a craving for physical pleasure, a craving for everything we see, and pride in our achievements and possessions. These are not from the Father, but are from this world.*

Satan is alive and active, and his legions of demons are always on the attack. A battle rages in the spiritual realm— a battle you can't see but one you will experience if you seek to serve God. You need God's power, not your own, to stand strong and not allow temptation to overcome you. Most of all, since you do not always know or understand the evil that is threatening you, you need God's power to give you strength to face an unknown enemy. Have peace that God has already won the battle over death and has the power to save you in this battle as well.

EQUALITY

Does God view all people equally?

GENESIS 1:27 | *God created human beings in his own image. In the image of God he created them; male and female he created them.*

PROVERBS 22:2 | *The rich and poor have this in common: The LORD made them both.*

All people are created by God, in the image of God, and have equal value in the eyes of God.

JOHN 3:16 | *God loved the world so much that he gave his one and only Son, so that everyone who believes in him will not perish but have eternal life.*

ACTS 10:34-35 | *God shows no favoritism. In every nation he accepts those who fear him and do what is right.*

ROMANS 3:22-24 | *We are made right with God by placing our faith in Jesus Christ. And this is true for everyone who believes, no matter who we are. For everyone has sinned; we all fall short of God's glorious standard. Yet God, with undeserved kindness, declares that we are righteous. He did this through Christ Jesus when he freed us from the penalty for our sins.*

ROMANS 5:18 | *Adam's one sin brings condemnation for everyone, but Christ's one act of righteousness brings a right relationship with God and new life for everyone.*

God's salvation is available to everyone. It doesn't matter what sins you've committed and it doesn't matter who you are. God loves all people equally and wants to see everyone saved from eternal death and living in relationship with him. When you decide to follow Jesus Christ and ask him to forgive your sins and make you a new person inside, he promises to look at you as though you've never sinned.

2 CORINTHIANS 5:10 | *We must all stand before Christ to be judged. We will each receive whatever we deserve for the good or evil we have done in this earthly body.*

COLOSSIANS 3:25 | *If you do what is wrong, you will be paid back for the wrong you have done. For God has no favorites.*

1 PETER 1:17 | *The heavenly Father to whom you pray has no favorites. He will judge or reward you according to what you do. So you must live in reverent fear of him.*

God will determine punishment or reward as he judges each person equally and individually.

ESCAPE

What can I do when I feel I can't escape Satan's temptations?

1 CORINTHIANS 10:13 | *The temptations in your life are no different from what others experience. And God is faithful. He will not allow the temptation to be more than you can stand. When you are tempted, he will show you a way out so that you can endure.*

Don't underestimate the power of Satan, but don't over-estimate it either. He can tempt you, but he cannot force you to sin. He can dangle the bait in front of you, but he cannot make you take it. The Bible promises that no temptation will ever be too strong for you to resist because, even in times of heavy temptation, God provides a way out. In those times, the Holy Spirit gives you the power and the wisdom to find the way of escape.

ETERNAL LIFE

Will eternal life with God be boring? Why should I look forward to living with him forever?

ECCLESIASTES 3:11 | *God has made everything beautiful for its own time. He has planted eternity in the human heart, but even so, people cannot see the whole scope of God's work from beginning to end.*

1 CORINTHIANS 2:9 | *No eye has seen, no ear has heard, and no mind has imagined what God has prepared for those who love him.*

King Solomon wrote in the book of Ecclesiastes that God has planted eternity in the human heart. This means that you innately know there is more than just this life—something you were made for is still missing. Because you were created in God's image, you have eternal value, and nothing but the eternal God can truly satisfy the desires of your heart. He has built into you a restless yearning for the kind of perfect world that can be found only in heaven. Through nature, art, and relationships, he gives you a glimpse of that world. Someday he will restore earth to the way it was when he first created it—when it was perfect—and eternity will be a never-ending exploration of earth's beauty and of the perfect relationship you'll have with God.

2 CORINTHIANS 5:1 | *We know that when this earthly tent we live in is taken down (that is, when we die and leave this earthly body), we will have a house in heaven, an eternal body made for us by God himself and not by human hands.*

REVELATION 21:3-4 | *Look, God's home is now among his people! He will live with them, and they will be his people. God himself will be with them. He will wipe every tear from their eyes, and there will be no more death or sorrow or crying or pain. All these things are gone forever.*

Eternity is not an extension of life here on earth, where you suffer, grieve, and hurt. Instead, God promises something new. He will restore this earth to be the way he once created it—as a beautiful place with no sin, sorrow, or pain. You will live in the world you long for without evil and suffering. God created humans for this earth, so the new earth will have a lot of similarities to this one, but it will be better and more amazing in every way. You will be in God's presence, forever filled with joy. You don't have to worry about simply strumming a harp on some cloud—there will be plenty to do that will be fun, fulfilling, and purposeful.

How can I be certain that there is eternal life?

JOHN 3:16 | *God loved the world so much that he gave his one and only Son, so that everyone who believes in him will not perish but have eternal life.*

1 CORINTHIANS 15:4-6 | *He was buried, and he was raised from the dead on the third day, just as the Scriptures said. He was seen by Peter and then by the Twelve. After that, he was seen*

by more than 500 of his followers at one time, most of whom are still alive, though some have died.

1 CORINTHIANS 15:20 | *Christ has been raised from the dead. He is the first of a great harvest of all who have died.*

1 CORINTHIANS 15:40, 42 | *The glory of the heavenly bodies is different from the glory of the earthly bodies. . . . It is the same way with the resurrection of the dead. Our earthly bodies are planted in the ground when we die, but they will be raised to live forever.*

The resurrection of Jesus is not mere religious lore. The biblical record mentions eyewitnesses to the risen Jesus and others who interviewed them. Historical investigation serves only to confirm the fact of the Resurrection. This, in turn, assures you of your eternal life. God promised the death and resurrection of Jesus, and he has promised the resurrection of your body after you die. If it happened to Jesus, as God said it would, then you can be assured of his promise to do the same for all who believe in him.

EVIL

If God is good, why does he let people do evil things? Why does a loving, sovereign God allow injustice? Why doesn't he stop it?

GENESIS 2:15-17 | *The LORD God placed the man in the Garden of Eden to tend and watch over it. But the LORD God warned him, "You may freely eat the fruit of every tree in the garden— except the tree of the knowledge of good and evil. If you eat its fruit, you are sure to die."*

Genuine love requires the freedom to choose. From the beginning, God desired a loving relationship with humans, so he gave them this freedom. But with the ability to make choices comes the possibility that people would choose their own way over God's way, which always leads to sin because all people are born with a sinful nature (see Romans 3:23). This breaks God's heart, but the alternative would have been to create robotlike humans who didn't choose to love God on their own. This state of affairs will end on the final Judgment Day. On that day, the people who chose to love God and accept what his Son, Jesus Christ, did for them—even though they have all sinned—will be taken into heaven because they showed during their lives that they wanted to live with him and love him for eternity.

PSALM 73:17-19 | *I went into your sanctuary, O God, and I finally understood the destiny of the wicked. Truly, you put them on a slippery path and send them sliding over the cliff to destruction. In an instant they are destroyed, completely swept away by terrors.*

Sometimes it seems that evil people can do anything they want and not only get away with it but flourish. God has promised, however, that one day everyone will be judged, evil will be exposed, and the righteous will prevail. If righteousness always prevailed on earth, then people wouldn't be following God for the right reasons—they would follow God only to have an easy life.

God doesn't promise the absence of evil on this earth. In fact, he warns that evil will be pervasive and powerful. But God promises to help you stand against evil, and if you do, you will receive your reward of eternal life with him in heaven, where evil will be no more.

How do I fight against evil?

EPHESIANS 6:10-11, 16 | *Be strong in the Lord and in his mighty power. Put on all of God's armor. . . . Hold up the shield of faith to stop the fiery arrows of the devil.*

COLOSSIANS 2:15 | *He disarmed the spiritual rulers and authorities. He shamed them publicly by his victory over them on the cross.*

1 JOHN 4:4 | *You belong to God. . . . You have already won a victory . . . because the Spirit who lives in you is greater than the spirit who lives in the world.*

1 JOHN 5:4 | *Every child of God defeats this evil world, and we achieve this victory through our faith.*

Your first line of defense is to draw strength from the fact that God is more powerful than your problems and your enemies. Your faith in God is like a shield that protects you from the temptations and criticisms hurled at you every day. Without strong faith, the weapons of Satan and the arrows shot at you by your enemies would pierce and defeat you. So even when life seems overwhelming, use your faith like a shield and you will withstand the dangers and discouragements you face. And rejoice because God has already won the victory.

1 CORINTHIANS 10:12-13 | *If you think you are standing strong, be careful not to fall. The temptations in your life are no different from what others experience. And God is faithful. He will not allow the temptation to be more than you can stand. When you are tempted, he will show you a way out so that you can endure.*

Stop giving in to temptation. God's Word makes it clear that sin always hurts you because it separates you from God (your source of mercy and blessing) and puts you in the clutches of the enemy. Giving in to temptation puts you right in the middle of the road where evil hurtles toward you at high speed. Being run over by the consequences of sin will cause great distress in your life. The next time you find yourself facing something you know is wrong, get off the road of temptation before the consequences of sin run you over. God has promised to give you the strength to resist temptation if you ask.

ROMANS 13:14 I *Clothe yourself with the presence of the Lord Jesus Christ. And don't let yourself think about ways to indulge your evil desires.*

Surrender yourself to Christ's control—the closer you walk with Christ, the harder it is to be caught in the snare of evil. And avoid situations where you know your resolve for righteousness will be tested.

EXPECTATIONS

What are some things I can expect in my relationship with God?

ISAIAH 55:8 I *"My thoughts are nothing like your thoughts," says the LORD. "And my ways are far beyond anything you could imagine."*

God often does the opposite of what you expect. He chose David to be king of Israel, the youngest son of Jesse rather than choosing the oldest. He took Saul, the most vicious opponent of the early church, and transformed him into Paul, the greatest and most courageous missionary of all time. He used a crucifixion, the sign of ultimate defeat, and made it the ultimate victory over sin and death for all eternity. Don't limit God to the horizon of your own under-standing and expectations. He wants to surprise you in ways that inspire your awe, love, gratitude, and joy. When something really good happens to you, do you feel lucky? Instead, feel blessed by recognizing that your good fortune is from the hand of God. Only when you believe he is acting on your behalf will your relationship with him grow to a deeper level.

AMOS 5:24 | *[The Lord says,] "I want to see a mighty flood of justice, an endless river of righteous living."*

JAMES 1:5-7 | *If you need wisdom, ask our generous God, and he will give it to you. He will not rebuke you for asking. But when you ask him, be sure that your faith is in God alone. Do not waver, for a person with divided loyalty is as unsettled as a wave of the sea that is blown and tossed by the wind. Such people should not expect to receive anything from the Lord.*

Sometimes it might seem as if God places unrealistic expectations on you. How can you possibly obey all that he commands? How can you love according to his standards? God understands that humanly speaking these expectations are impossible, but with his help, they become possible. God's greatest expectation is not that you live a perfect life, but that you love him with all your heart. Understanding that God doesn't expect you to be perfect but, rather, applauds you when you sincerely try to follow him becomes a holy moment in which you no longer see him as a strict taskmaster but a loving encourager.

FAITH

What is faith?

JOHN 5:24 | *[Jesus said,] "I tell you the truth, those who listen to my message and believe in God who sent me have eternal life."*

ACTS 16:31 | *Believe in the Lord Jesus and you will be saved.*

HEBREWS 11:1 | *Faith is the confidence that what we hope for will actually happen; it gives us assurance about things we cannot see.*

Faith is more than just believing; it is trusting your very life to what you believe. You can believe that someone can walk across a deep gorge on a tightrope. But are you willing to trust that person to carry you across? Faith would say yes. Faith in God means that you are willing to trust him to carry you across the tightrope of life. You are willing to follow his guidelines for living as outlined in the Bible because you have the conviction that this will be best for you. You are even willing to endure ridicule and persecution for your faith because you are sure that God is who he says he is and that he will keep his promises about his love for you, about his help in times of trouble, about his salvation for all who believe, and about eternal life in heaven.

Faith seems so complicated; how can I ever understand it?

MARK 5:36 | *Jesus . . . said to Jairus, "Don't be afraid. Just have faith."*

Too often people make faith difficult, but that wasn't what Jesus intended. Faith isn't complicated. It simply means trusting Jesus to do what he has promised.

How much faith must I have?

MATTHEW 17:20 | *[Jesus said,] "I tell you the truth, if you had faith even as small as a mustard seed, you could say to this mountain, 'Move from here to there,' and it would move. Nothing would be impossible."*

The mustard seed was often used to illustrate the smallest seed known to people. Jesus said that faith is not a matter of size or quantity. It is not the size of your faith but the size of the One in whom you believe that makes the difference. You do not have to have great faith in God; rather you have faith in a great God.

How does faith in God affect my life?

GENESIS 15:6 | *Abram believed the LORD, and the LORD counted him as righteous because of his faith.*

ROMANS 3:24-25 | *God, with undeserved kindness, declares that we are righteous. He did this through Christ Jesus when he freed us from the penalty for our sins. . . . People are made right with God when they believe that Jesus sacrificed his life, shedding his blood.*

Faith is your lifeline to God. Sin breaks your relationship with God—cutting your lifeline to him. A holy God cannot live with unholy people. But the simple act of faith when you accept Jesus as Savior and ask him to forgive your sins makes you holy in God's sight, restoring your lifeline to him.

ROMANS 8:5 | *Those who are dominated by the sinful nature think about sinful things, but those who are controlled by the Holy Spirit think about things that please the Spirit.*

1 CORINTHIANS 12:1 | *Brothers and sisters, regarding your question about the special abilities the Spirit gives us. . . .*

GALATIANS 5:22 | *The Holy Spirit produces this kind of fruit in our lives: . . . faithfulness.*

Faith is inviting God's Holy Spirit to live in you. It is not just an act of the mind; it taps you into the very resources of God so that you have the power to live in an entirely new way—a way that is happy and joyful and has ultimate meaning.

1 THESSALONIANS 3:7-8 | *We have been greatly encouraged in the midst of our troubles and suffering, dear brothers and sisters, because you have remained strong in your faith. It gives us new life to know that you are standing firm in the Lord.*

Like a muscle, faith gets stronger the more you exercise it. When you do what God asks you to do and then see him bless you as a result of your obedience, your faith grows stronger. And when others see your faith growing stronger, they are encouraged and greatly motivated to grow stronger in their faith as well.

FAITHFULNESS

Why should I be faithful to God?

1 SAMUEL 17:45-46, 50 | *David [said] to the Philistine, "You come to me with sword, spear, and javelin, but I come to you in the name of the LORD of Heaven's Armies—the God of the armies of Israel, whom you have defied. Today the LORD will conquer you. . . . So David triumphed over the Philistine with only a sling and a stone, for he had no sword.*

ACTS 4:13 | *The members of the council were amazed when they saw the boldness of Peter and John, for they could see that they were ordinary men with no special training in the Scriptures. They also recognized them as men who had been with Jesus.*

God chooses to accomplish great deeds through faithful people.

PSALM 1:1-3 | *Oh, the joys of those who do not follow the advice of the wicked, or stand around with sinners, or join in with mockers. But they delight in the law of the LORD, meditating on it day and night. They are like trees planted along the riverbank, bearing fruit each season. Their leaves never wither, and they prosper in all they do.*

Faithfulness determines the quality of your character, which affects the quality of your life, bringing vitality and productivity.

PROVERBS 3:3-4 | *Never let loyalty and kindness leave you! . . . Then you will find favor with both God and people, and you will earn a good reputation.*

Faithfulness is an essential characteristic of a reputation that others can trust. When there are problems, sometimes your faithfulness is the key to a positive outcome.

2 TIMOTHY 2:11-13 | *This is a trustworthy saying: If we die with him, we will also live with him. If we endure hardship, we will reign with him. If we deny him, he will deny us. If we are unfaithful, he remains faithful, for he cannot deny who he is.*

Faithfulness is an essential part of love. Despite your sins, God loves you and remains faithful to you. Model the love of Christ to others and remain faithful to them, even when they fail you.

REVELATION 2:10 | *If you remain faithful even when facing death, I will give you the crown of life.*

Faithfulness brings eternal rewards.

HEBREWS 3:14 | *If we are faithful to the end, . . . we will share in all that belongs to Christ.*

There is nothing like the faithfulness of others to build your sense of security. And there is nothing like the faithfulness of God to build your confidence in your eternal security.

FALSE TEACHING

How can I keep from being deceived by false teaching?

JOHN 10:3-5 | *[Jesus said,] "The gatekeeper opens the gate for him, and the sheep recognize his voice and come to him. . . . After he has gathered his own flock, he walks ahead of them, and they follow him because they know his voice. They won't follow a stranger; they will run from him because they don't know his voice."*

Jesus says in these verses that when you really know someone, you can instantly recognize his or her voice. You can pick it out in a crowd because it is unique and distinct. In the same way, as you spend time studying the teachings of Jesus and getting to know him better in prayer, you will get to know his voice. And when people are preaching or teaching, you will be able to recognize if what they are saying is consistent with what Jesus would say.

1 TIMOTHY 4:6 | *If you explain these things to the brothers and sisters, Timothy, you will be a worthy servant of Christ Jesus, one who is nourished by the message of faith and the good teaching you have followed.*

The only way for you to stand your ground as a believer is to be spiritually fit. Are you consistently exposing yourself to solid teaching, or are you leaving your spiritual formation to chance?

JAMES 3:1 | *Dear brothers and sisters, not many of you should become teachers in the church, for we who teach will be judged more strictly.*

Carefully evaluate your spiritual teachers. Are they people of high moral character? Does what they say cause you to love Jesus more, or to admire them instead? Are they humble? Do they teach truths that are consistent with the Bible?

COLOSSIANS 2:8 | *Don't let anyone capture you with empty philosophies and high-sounding nonsense that come from*

*human thinking and from the spiritual powers of this world,
rather than from Christ.*

1 JOHN 4:1 | *Do not believe everyone who claims to speak by the
Spirit. You must test them to see if the spirit they have comes
from God. For there are many false prophets in the world.*

By knowing God and his truth, found in the Bible, you
will be able to recognize the devil's attempts to offer
what seems to be good but really leads only to hurt and
disastrous consequences.

FEAR OF GOD

What does it mean to fear God?

PSALM 33:8 | *Let the whole world fear the LORD, and let every-
one stand in awe of him.*

PROVERBS 9:10 | *Fear of the LORD is the foundation of wisdom.*

Fearing God is not the same as being afraid of God.
Being afraid of someone drives you away from him or her.
Fearing God means being awed by his power and goodness, drawing you closer to him and to the blessings he
gives. Fearing God is like the respect you have for beloved
teachers, coaches, parents, or mentors who motivate you
to do your best, so you avoid doing anything that would
offend them or provoke their displeasure. A healthy fear
should drive you to God for forgiveness and help you
keep your perspective about where you need to be in
your relationship with him.

How can fearing God make me joyful?

PSALM 2:11 | *Serve the LORD with reverent fear, and rejoice with trembling.*

PSALM 128:1 | *How joyful are those who fear the LORD—all who follow his ways!*

ISAIAH 41:10 | *Don't be afraid, for I am with you. Don't be discouraged, for I am your God. I will strengthen you and help you. I will hold you up with my victorious right hand.*

How interesting that those who fear the Lord actually experience more joy! Because God is so great and mighty and because he holds the power of life and death in his hands, you should have a healthy, reverent fear of him. A healthy fear of God recognizes what he could do if he gave you what you deserved. This *would* be the same as being afraid of his hurting you *if* he didn't promise to always love and protect you. But he does love you, and he gives you mercy and forgiveness. Thus, a healthy fear should drive you *to* God in thankfulness, for forgiveness, and in awe that he wants a loving relationship with you. You fear God because of his awesome power; you love God for the way he blesses you with it. And this brings great joy.

FELLOWSHIP

Why do I need fellowship with other believers?

MATTHEW 18:20 | *[Jesus said,] "Where two or three gather together as my followers, I am there among them."*

ACTS 11:23 | *When he arrived and saw this evidence of God's blessing, he was filled with joy, and he encouraged the believers to stay true to the Lord.*

ROMANS 12:5 | *We are many parts of one body, and we all belong to each other.*

COLOSSIANS 3:16 | *Teach and counsel each other with all the wisdom he gives. Sing psalms and hymns and spiritual songs to God with thankful hearts.*

1 JOHN 1:7 | *If we are living in the light, as God is in the light, then we have fellowship with each other, and the blood of Jesus, his Son, cleanses us from all sin.*

God created you for relationship. You cannot grow as a believer all by yourself, without other Christians around you. Fellowship among believers in Jesus (at church or in small groups) is unique because it invites the living God into your group. You gather with people who have a common perspective on life, a belief that your sins have been forgiven, affecting your freedom and your future. Christian fellowship provides a place for honest sharing about the things in life that really matter, encouragement to stay strong in the face of temptation and persecution, and supernatural help in dealing with problems.

FOLLOWING

What does it mean to follow Jesus?

MATTHEW 19:27 | *Peter said to [Jesus], "We've given up everything to follow you."*

LUKE 14:27 | *[Jesus said,] "If you do not carry your own cross and follow me, you cannot be my disciple."*

Following Jesus means leaving behind anything that might take your focus off him and devoting yourself to him with all your heart. Thinking less about what you are giving up and more about the blessings and benefits will make following Jesus desirable.

LUKE 5:11 | *As soon as they landed, they left everything and followed Jesus.*

Following Jesus means more than acknowledging him as Savior. It means reorienting your life so that, no matter what you do, you do it as service to him. For example, if you are in sales, you view selling as a means to supply people's needs with fairness and integrity.

MATTHEW 16:24 | *Jesus said to his disciples, "If any of you wants to be my follower, you must turn from your selfish ways, take up your cross, and follow me."*

Following Jesus is not a sentimental experience, but a costly commitment. Following Jesus must be more than a hobby, more than a part-time activity. His love is too wonderful and his work is too important for anything less than your complete devotion.

MATTHEW 5:16 | *Let your good deeds shine out for all to see, so that everyone will praise your heavenly Father.*

When you claim to be a follower of God, make sure others can truly see you following him. They will want to follow when they like what they see.

FORGIVENESS

What does it really mean to be forgiven?

ISAIAH 1:18 | *The LORD [said,] "Though your sins are like scarlet, I will make them as white as snow. Though they are red like crimson, I will make them as white as wool."*

COLOSSIANS 1:22 | *[God] has reconciled you to himself through the death of Christ. . . . As a result, he has brought you into his own presence, and you are holy and blameless as you stand before him without a single fault.*

Forgiveness means that God looks at you as though you had never sinned. When you receive his forgiveness, you are blameless before him. When God forgives, he doesn't sweep your sins under the carpet; instead, he completely washes them away.

ROMANS 4:7 | *Oh, what joy for those whose disobedience is forgiven, whose sins are put out of sight.*

COLOSSIANS 2:13 | *You were dead because of your sins and because your sinful nature was not yet cut away. Then God made you alive with Christ, for he forgave all our sins.*

Forgiveness brings great joy because you have been freed from the heavy weight of guilt and you are no longer a slave to your sinful nature.

ACTS 2:38 | *Each of you must repent of your sins and turn to God, and be baptized in the name of Jesus Christ for the forgiveness of your sins. Then you will receive the gift of the Holy Spirit.*

Forgiveness of sins allows you to receive the gift of God's Holy Spirit. The Holy Spirit taps you into the very power of God to help you battle temptation and to guide you through life.

ROMANS 10:9-10 | *If you confess with your mouth that Jesus is Lord and believe in your heart that God raised him from the dead, you will be saved. For it is by believing in your heart that you are made right with God, and it is by confessing with your mouth that you are saved.*

Forgiveness is the only way you can have the assurance of eternal life in heaven.

How can I possibly forgive those who have greatly hurt me?

MATTHEW 6:12 | *Forgive us our sins, as we have forgiven those who sin against us.*

LUKE 6:37 | *Do not judge others, and you will not be judged. Do not condemn others, or it will all come back against you. Forgive others, and you will be forgiven.*

LUKE 23:34 | *Jesus said, "Father, forgive them, for they don't know what they are doing."*

EPHESIANS 4:32 | *Be kind to each other, tenderhearted, forgiving one another, just as God through Christ has forgiven you.*

Just as God has forgiven you, even though you didn't deserve it, you must forgive others, even though they don't deserve it. That is what God's forgiveness is all about—it is complete and undeserved. Only then can forgiveness work its miraculous healing power. Forgiveness is a choice, a commitment to reflect God's love to others.

ROMANS 3:24 | *God, with undeserved kindness, declares that we are righteous. He did this through Christ Jesus when he freed us from the penalty for our sins.*

COLOSSIANS 3:13 | *Make allowance for each other's faults, and forgive anyone who offends you. Remember, the Lord forgave you, so you must forgive others.*

Forgiveness is a command, not an option. It is necessary for your own health and your relationship with God. Jesus gave you the perfect example of forgiveness. Forgiveness doesn't mean you say that the hurt doesn't exist or that it doesn't matter, nor does it make everything "all right." Rather, it allows you to let go of the hurt and let God deal with the one who hurt you. Forgiveness sets you free and allows you to move on with your life. It's not always easy, but forgiving others who have caused you hurt is the healthiest act you can do for yourself.

FREEDOM

Why did God give me the freedom to choose or reject him and his commands?

DEUTERONOMY 11:26-28 | *[Moses said,] "Look, today I am giving you the choice between a blessing and a curse! You will be blessed if you obey the commands of the LORD your God that I am giving you today. But you will be cursed if you reject the commands of the LORD your God and turn away from him and worship gods you have not known before."*

It sounds contradictory, but evil exists because God is loving. The Bible teaches that God created human beings with the freedom to choose to love and obey him and do what is right—or to disregard him and disobey and do what is wrong. God gave the gift of freedom because without freedom there can be no love. God could have created you that you could do only good—therefore eliminating the possibility of evil—but you would then be a machine without the capacity to choose or to love. Only when you choose to love does it become real.

FRUIT OF THE SPIRIT

What does the Bible mean when it says my life should produce "fruit"?

LUKE 6:44-45 | *A tree is identified by its fruit. . . . A good person produces good things from the treasury of a good heart, and an evil person produces evil things from the treasury of an evil heart. What you say flows from what is in your heart.*

JOHN 15:5 | *[Jesus said,] "I am the vine; you are the branches. Those who remain in me, and I in them, will produce much fruit. For apart from me you can do nothing."*

GALATIANS 5:22-23 | *The Holy Spirit produces this kind of fruit in our lives: love, joy, peace, patience, kindness, goodness, faithfulness, gentleness, and self-control.*

The "fruit" the Bible talks about is the "fruit of the Spirit," character qualities that the Holy Spirit wants you to allow him to develop in your life. But he will not force you to have these qualities. When you accept Jesus as Savior, the Holy Spirit literally comes to live in you. Only he has the power to put your old nature to death (see Romans 8:9), giving you a new nature that produces good fruit, or good character traits. Your life will continue to bear good fruit only as you stay connected to the source of growth.

FUN

Can I be a Christian and still have fun?

NEHEMIAH 8:10 | *Go and celebrate with a feast . . . and share gifts of food with people who have nothing prepared. This is a sacred day. . . . Don't be . . . sad, for the joy of the LORD is your strength!*

PROVERBS 13:9 | *The life of the godly is full of light and joy, but the light of the wicked will be snuffed out.*

ECCLESIASTES 3:1, 4 | *For everything there is a season, a time for every activity under heaven. . . . A time to cry and a time to laugh. A time to grieve and a time to dance.*

MATTHEW 25:21 | *You have been faithful in handling this small amount. . . . Let's celebrate together!*

Following God doesn't exclude fun. Following God's commandments is the way to get the most out of life—enjoying life as it was originally created to be enjoyed. God wants you to have fun, to enjoy others, and to find joy in your relationship with him. Joy, fun, and celebration are important parts of believing in God because they lift your spirits and help you see the beauty and meaning in life. These enjoyable experiences give you a small taste of the joy you will experience in heaven. Following God's way keeps

you from experiencing the sad and hurtful consequences
of sin, which allows you to better enjoy all the gifts and
benefits of life as it was meant to be lived.

FUTURE

Why doesn't God reveal more of the future to me, as one of his followers?

ISAIAH 14:24 | *The LORD of Heaven's Armies has sworn this
oath: "It will all happen as I have planned. It will be as I
have decided."*

1 CORINTHIANS 2:9 | *No eye has seen, no ear has heard, and no mind
has imagined what God has prepared for those who love him.*

God reveals enough to give you hope. You know there is a
heaven, you know how to get to heaven, and you know that
your future in heaven will be more wonderful than you can
imagine. Perhaps to know any more than that would be
beyond your finite understanding—the rest requires faith.

GENESIS 12:1-2, 4 | *The LORD had said to Abram, "Leave your
native country, your relatives, and your father's family, and go to
the land that I will show you. I will make you into a great nation.
I will bless you and make you famous, and you will be a blessing to
others." . . . So Abram departed as the LORD had instructed.*

JOHN 21:22 | *Jesus [said], "If I want him to remain alive until
I return, what is that to you? As for you, follow me."*

God reveals enough to encourage you to obey. Achieving
God's future rewards requires your present obedience.

JAMES 4:10 | *Humble yourselves before the Lord, and he will lift you up in honor.*

JAMES 4:13-16 | *Look here, you who say, "Today or tomorrow we are going to a certain town and will stay there a year. We will do business there and make a profit." How do you know what your life will be like tomorrow? Your life is like the morning fog—it's here a little while, then it's gone. What you ought to say is, "If the Lord wants us to, we will live and do this or that." Otherwise you are boasting about your own plans, and all such boasting is evil.*

God reveals enough to increase your dependence on him. He knows your future, and he wants to be part of that future, so you must rely on him to lead you there. That is the essence of what it means to live by faith. Faith is trusting God for your future, not trying to create it all by yourself.

I'm afraid that if I trust God, he will "take" me someplace I don't want to go. What can I do about this fear?

PSALM 20:4 | *May he grant your heart's desires and make all your plans succeed.*

PSALM 37:4 | *Take delight in the LORD, and he will give you your heart's desires.*

PSALM 103:5 | *He fills my life with good things.*

JEREMIAH 29:11 | *"I know the plans I have for you," says the LORD. "They are plans for good and not for disaster, to give you a future and a hope."*

JOHN 10:10 | *[Jesus said,] "My purpose is to give them a rich and satisfying life."*

God's plans are always good plans. His desires for you will fulfill and satisfy you. If your mind and heart are truly in tune with his will, you won't be going where you don't want to go: He changes your heart before he adjusts your future plans. Will you let him change your heart? Since God alone knows the future, who can plan for it better than he?

GIVING

Why is generosity important to God?

MATTHEW 6:21 | *Wherever your treasure is, there the desires of your heart will also be.*

Who is more generous—a billionaire who gives one million dollars to his church or a poor, single parent who gives one hundred dollars? If someone has—and keeps—a lot of money, does that mean he or she is not generous? Jesus said the answer to those questions cannot be known without knowing the heart of the giver. Throughout the Bible, God doesn't focus on how much money you have but rather on how generous you are with it. One thing is clear: Wherever your money goes reveals what you care most about. Realizing that everything you have is a gift from a generous God motivates you to share your possessions more freely.

MALACHI 3:10 | *"Bring all the tithes into the storehouse so there will be enough food in my Temple. If you do," says the LORD of Heaven's Armies, "I will open the windows of heaven for you. I will pour out a blessing so great you won't have enough room to take it in! Try it! Put me to the test!"*

Old Testament law made it clear that God wanted his people to tithe—to give him the first tenth of their harvest and herds and income—to demonstrate obedience and trust that he would provide for them. When Jesus came, he made it clear that he loves a cheerful giver. This means that he loves a generous heart. The principle of the tithe is a good place to start as you set an example for those you lead. It demonstrates generosity to those in need, commitment to being a part of God's bigger work in the world, and sacrifice in order to give more to others. God promises to bless that kind of faithful giving, which inspires others to give faithfully as well.

HEBREWS 13:16 | *Don't forget to do good and to share with those in need. These are the sacrifices that please God.*

Generosity is both a spiritual gift and a spiritual discipline. Generosity is an important character trait to God because it is the opposite of selfishness, which along with pride, is one of the most destructive sins. Selfishness promotes greed, stinginess, envy, and hard-heartedness—all traits that destroy relationships. Generosity promotes giving, trusting, being merciful, and putting the needs of others above your own—all traits that build relationships.

GOD'S PLAN FOR YOU

Did God really want me to be born? Does he have a plan for me?

PSALM 139:13-16 | *You made all the delicate, inner parts of my body and knit me together in my mother's womb. Thank you for making me so wonderfully complex! Your workmanship is marvelous—how well I know it. You watched me as I was being formed in utter seclusion, as I was woven together in the dark of the womb. You saw me before I was born. Every day of my life was recorded in your book. Every moment was laid out before a single day had passed.*

JEREMIAH 1:5 | *I knew you before I formed you in your mother's womb. Before you were born I set you apart.*

God not only knew all about you before you were born but wanted you to be born, and he has a plan for your life.

PSALM 139:3 | *You see me when I travel and when I rest at home. You know everything I do.*

The Bible talks about God's having both a general plan and a specific plan for your life. He wants you to follow a certain path toward his desired purpose for you, but he also cares about the details along the way. In both the big and the small picture, God shows his love and care.

PSALM 138:8 | *The LORD will work out his plans for my life.*

PHILIPPIANS 1:6 | *I am certain that God, who began the good work within you, will continue his work until it is finally finished on the day when Christ Jesus returns.*

God's plan for your life is not an unthinking, automated script that you must follow. It is a journey with various important destinations and appointments, but also a great deal of freedom as to the pace and scope of the travel. God's plan for you will always have a sense of mystery, but you can be certain that he will guide you as long as you rely on his leading.

JEREMIAH 29:11 | *"I know the plans I have for you," says the LORD. "They are plans for good and not for disaster, to give you a future and a hope."*

Sometimes you might be tempted to question God's will for your life, thinking he has made a mistake. Ultimately, what looks like a mistake to you now will be God's means to bring about something fulfilling and wonderful.

Has God called me to do specific things?

JEREMIAH 1:4-5 | *The LORD gave me this message: "I knew you before I formed you in your mother's womb. Before you were born I set you apart."*

God may call you to do a certain job or to accomplish a very specific task or ministry. When that happens, he will make sure you know what it is—you will feel a very strong sense of leading from him. It's up to you to respond and walk through the door of opportunity he opens.

1 CORINTHIANS 12:4, 7 | *There are different kinds of spiritual gifts, but the same Spirit is the source of them all. . . . A spiritual gift is given to each of us so we can help each other.*

2 TIMOTHY 4:5 | *Fully carry out the ministry God has given you.*

God gives each individual a spiritual gift (sometimes more than one!) and a special ministry in the church. You can use your gifts to help and encourage others and to bring glory to God's name. These specific spiritual gifts help you fulfill the purpose for which he made you.

1 CORINTHIANS 7:24 | *Each of you, dear brothers and sisters, should remain as you were when God first called you.*

The call to follow Jesus does not necessarily mean a call to a specific job or Christian ministry. Sometimes your call may simply be to obey God wherever you are right now.

ECCLESIASTES 11:9 | *Do everything you want to do; take it all in. But remember that you must give an account to God for everything you do.*

God gives you the freedom to follow many different roads over the course of your life and to pursue many different activities, but remember that you will have to answer to him for everything you do. Not everything you do is a call from God, but everything you do is accountable to God.

GOVERNMENT

What does God say about the government?

ROMANS 13:1-2 | *Everyone must submit to governing authorities. For all authority comes from God, and those in positions of authority have been placed there by God. So anyone who rebels against authority is rebelling against what God has instituted.*

The Bible says it is important to obey those in authority over you.

ACTS 4:19; 5:29 | *Peter and John [said], "Do you think God wants us to obey you rather than him? . . . We must obey God rather than any human authority."*

Unless those in authority order you to denounce God or to deliberately disobey him, you must follow their orders. But God is the highest authority, and you must obey him first and above all else.

GRACE

What is the grace of God?

ROMANS 6:23 | *The wages of sin is death, but the free gift of God is eternal life through Christ Jesus our Lord.*

EPHESIANS 2:8-9 | *God saved you by his grace when you believed. And you can't take credit for this; it is a gift from God. Salvation is not a reward for the good things we have done, so none of us can boast about it.*

HEBREWS 4:16 | *Let us come boldly to the throne of our gracious God. There we will receive his mercy, and we will find grace to help us when we need it most.*

Grace is a big favor you do for someone without expecting anything in return. When the Bible says you are saved by grace, it means that God has done you the biggest favor of all: He has pardoned you from the death sentence you deserve for sinning against him. You do not have to earn God's grace, nor work your way to heaven. By grace, you are forgiven for your sins and restored to full fellowship with God. Like the gift of life itself, you cannot take credit for it—any more than a baby can brag about being born! The fact that this is God's gift and not the product of your own effort gives you great comfort, security, and hope. The only stipulation to grace is that you must accept it as a gift; otherwise, you can't enjoy its benefits.

GUARDING YOUR HEART

How do I protect my heart from temptation?

PROVERBS 4:23 | *Guard your heart above all else, for it determines the course of your life.*

The intent of a guardrail on a dangerous curve is not to inhibit your freedom to drive but to save your life! In the same way, you need a "guardrail" as you travel through life, not to inhibit your freedom but to keep your life from going out of control. Your heart determines where you go because it is the part of you that most affects your passions and emotions. If you don't guard your heart with the boundaries explained in the Bible and stay focused on the road ahead where God wants you to go, you may have a terrible accident when temptation distracts you.

GUIDANCE

Will God tell me what he wants me to do for the rest of my life?

PSALM 32:8 | *The LORD says, "I will guide you along the best pathway for your life. I will advise you and watch over you."*

PSALM 119:105 | *Your word is a lamp to guide my feet and a light for my path.*

PSALM 138:8 | *The LORD will work out his plans for my life—for your faithful love, O LORD, endures forever.*

PROVERBS 3:5 | *Trust in the LORD with all your heart; do not depend on your own understanding.*

If you could see your future, you'd be either very scared of the hard times ahead or very cocky about your accomplishments. Instead of a searchlight that brightens a huge area, God's guidance is more like a flashlight that illumines just enough of the path ahead to show you where to take the next few steps. God usually doesn't reveal it all at once. He wants you to learn to trust him each step of the way.

GUILT

How can I stop feeling guilty about the bad things I do? How might feelings of guilt help me?

LEVITICUS 5:5 | *When you become aware of your guilt . . ., you must confess your sin.*

PSALM 19:12-13 | *Cleanse me from these hidden faults. Keep your servant from deliberate sins! Don't let them control me.*

PSALM 32:5 | *Finally, I confessed all my sins to you and stopped trying to hide my guilt. I said to myself, "I will confess my rebellion to the LORD." And you forgave me! All my guilt is gone.*

JEREMIAH 3:13 | *Acknowledge your guilt. Admit that you rebelled against the LORD your God.*

1 JOHN 1:9 | *If we confess our sins to him, he is faithful and just to forgive us our sins and to cleanse us.*

A guilty conscience is a warning signal God has placed inside you to tell you when you've done something wrong. God often uses the feeling of guilt to tell you it is the right time to apologize. You must not lose this important sense of guilt; otherwise, you will not know when you have hurt or offended God or someone else. Do you feel guilty about something you have said or done to hurt another person? Then now is the time to apologize and seek forgiveness. Act quickly so you do not become desensitized to your feelings of guilt. Ask God to reveal actions and thoughts that you aren't even aware displease him. Confession indicates your desire to make things right, to be forgiven. What results from your confession? God removes your guilt, God restores your joy, and God heals broken relationships with those you have wronged. No matter how often you fail God, as long as you seek forgiveness, you don't need to continue to feel guilty about what you've done, because God has already forgotten about it!

HAND OF GOD

Does God really act in my life? How can I do a better job of noticing what he is doing?

NEHEMIAH 2:17-18 | *I said to them, "You know very well what trouble we are in. Jerusalem lies in ruins, and its gates have been destroyed by fire. Let us rebuild the wall of Jerusalem and end this disgrace!" Then I told them about how the gracious hand of God had been on me, and about my conversation with the king. They replied at once, "Yes, let's rebuild the wall!" So they began the good work.*

PSALM 106:2 | *Who can list the glorious miracles of the LORD? Who can ever praise him enough?*

Maybe you think that whenever God does anything on this earth, it is a dramatic miracle, such as raising a person from the dead. But all around you are supernatural occurrences from the hand of God, maybe not as dramatic as the parting of the Red Sea, but no less powerful. The birth of a baby, the healing of an illness, the rebirth of the earth in spring, the gift of salvation by faith alone, the work of love and forgiveness that changes someone, the excitement of hearing the specific call of God in your life—these are just a few. If you think you've never seen the hand of God at work, look closer. He is active all around you.

HARD-HEARTEDNESS

What are the signs of a hard heart?

EXODUS 7:13 | *Pharaoh's heart, however, remained hard. He still refused to listen, just as the LORD had predicted.*

1 SAMUEL 1:15 | *[Hannah said,] "I haven't been drinking wine or anything stronger. But I am very discouraged, and I was pouring out my heart to the LORD."*

EZEKIEL 36:26 | *[The sovereign Lord said,] "I will give you a new heart, and I will put a new spirit in you. I will take out your stony, stubborn heart and give you a tender, responsive heart."*

LUKE 15:28-32 | *The older brother was angry and wouldn't go in. His father came out and begged him, but he replied, "All these years I've slaved for you and never once refused to do a single thing you told me to. And in all that time you never gave me even one young goat for a feast with my friends. Yet when this son of yours comes back after squandering your money on prostitutes, you celebrate by killing the fattened calf!" His father said to him, "Look, dear son, you have always stayed by me, and everything I have is yours. We had to celebrate this happy day. For your brother was dead and has come back to life! He was lost, but now he is found!"*

Pharaoh had a hard, stubborn heart. No matter how much he heard about God or how many miracles he saw, he refused to believe. The older brother of the Prodigal Son also struggled with a hard heart; he was more eager to punish than to forgive. As you evaluate the condition of your own heart, you must constantly ask if it is becoming harder and more stubborn or more open and pliable, reaching out to God whatever your circumstances. If you find it hard to forgive others when they ask for it or if you struggle to see God in your daily life, your heart may be in the process of hardening. If you let it continue, you cut yourself off from God, the only One who can really help you. A hard heart rejects the only thing that can save it—God's love. A soft heart will seek God's help and notice his perfectly timed responses.

HEAVEN

Is there really a heaven?

JOHN 14:2 | *There is more than enough room in my Father's home. If this were not so, would I have told you that I am going to prepare a place for you?*

2 CORINTHIANS 5:1 I *We know that when this earthly tent we live in is taken down (that is, when we die and leave this earthly body), we will have a house in heaven.*

Not only is there a heaven, but Jesus is making preparations for your arrival. Heaven is described most often in terms of being your home. It is not a paradise you will simply visit on vacation but an eternal dwelling place where you will live in joyful fellowship with your heavenly Father and all his family.

ECCLESIASTES 3:11 I *God has made everything beautiful for its own time. He has planted eternity in the human heart.*

God created you with an instinct for heaven, an inner longing to live forever. It is not just wishful thinking; it is God's intended purpose for you.

1 CORINTHIANS 15:20 I *Christ has been raised from the dead. He is the first of a great harvest of all who have died.*

Jesus' resurrection gives you the promise and assurance of your own resurrection to heaven and eternal life.

GENESIS 1:1, 9, 11, 20, 24, 27, 31 I *In the beginning God created the heavens and the earth. . . . Then God said, "Let the waters beneath the sky flow together into one place, so dry ground may appear." . . . Then God said, "Let the land sprout with vege-tation—every sort of seed-bearing plant, and trees." . . . Then God said, "Let the waters swarm with fish and other life. Let the skies be filled with birds of every kind." . . . Then God said, "Let the earth produce every sort of animal." . . . [Then] God created human beings in his own image . . . male and female he created them. . . . Then God looked over all he had made, and he saw that it was very good!*

2 PETER 3:13 | *We are looking forward to the new heavens and new earth he has promised, a world filled with God's righteousness.*

REVELATION 21:1 | *I saw a new heaven and a new earth.*

God originally created earth to be heaven—the place where he lived and walked and talked with Adam and Eve, side by side. Sin changed all that when it separated people from God and corrupted the earth. But the point is that God originally thought of heavenly paradise as a very physical place, with trees and plants, mountains and waterfalls, fruits and vegetables. The Bible consistently refers to the new heaven—the place where we will be reunited with God—as the new earth. The place where we will live with God forever will be very similar to the place where we live now. If God said the original earth he created was "very good," then the new earth he is preparing for us will be similar and familiar to us.

REVELATION 21:3-4 | *I heard a loud shout from the throne, saying, "Look, God's home is now among his people! He will live with them, and they will be his people. God himself will be with them. He will wipe every tear from their eyes, and there will be no more death or sorrow or crying or pain. All these things are gone forever."*

The promise of the Bible is that God will remove all the sin and struggles of this fallen world and create a new heaven and a new earth. The best this world has to offer can't even compare with the glory to come!

What will heaven be like?

1 JOHN 2:24-25 | *You must remain faithful to what you have been taught from the beginning. If you do, you will remain*

*in fellowship with the Son and with the Father. And in this
fellowship we enjoy the eternal life he promised us.*

In heaven, God will fulfill your deepest longings. Even
at its best, life on earth always leaves us a bit dissatisfied.
Experiences don't usually live up to expectations. Many
dreams go unfulfilled, and we long for so much more.
These longings confirm that our souls are anticipating
something beyond what this life can deliver. They give
you hope that the day will come when your disappointments will vanish, and you will receive your heart's desires.
Heaven is more than a matter of cosmic geography. The
essence of heaven is a relationship with the God who has
promised only the best for you and will spend an eternity delivering on that promise. It doesn't get any better
than that.

Does obedience to God get me into heaven?

GALATIANS 2:16 | *We know that a person is made right with
God by faith in Jesus Christ, not by obeying the law. And we
have believed in Christ Jesus, so that we might be made right
with God because of our faith in Christ, not because we have
obeyed the law. For no one will ever be made right with God
by obeying the law.*

HEBREWS 11:8 | *It was by faith that Abraham obeyed when God
called him.*

Obedience is motivated by faith, but obedience itself is not
the way to heaven; only faith in Jesus Christ as Savior will
get you to heaven. Obedience is the result of faith, not the
pathway to heaven.

How does my knowing about heaven affect my life now?

2 CORINTHIANS 4:17 | *Our present troubles are small and won't last very long. Yet they produce for us a glory that vastly outweighs them and will last forever!*

As a heaven-bound follower of Jesus, try to put heaven and earth in perspective. Here, you will probably live for less than a hundred years. In heaven, one hundred million years will be just the beginning. Yet amazingly, God determined that how you live during your short time on earth should prepare you for heaven. This gives purpose to life, perspective on your troubles, and anticipation for the unique role God has planned for you in eternity.

PHILIPPIANS 1:6 | *God, who began the good work within you, will continue his work until it is finally finished on the day when Christ Jesus returns.*

The key to perseverance on earth is having a clear view of heaven. When you see clearly where you are going, you can endure the hardships along the road.

In my life after I die, do I keep my body or get a new one, or do I have no body at all?

1 CORINTHIANS 15:40, 42 | *The glory of the heavenly bodies is different from the glory of the earthly bodies. . . . It is the same way with the resurrection of the dead. Our earthly bodies are planted in the ground when we die, but they will be raised to live forever.*

Your present body gets sick and will increasingly become a burden to you. It will age and deteriorate. You really wouldn't want to live in your present body forever. Think how many physical problems you would accumulate in a few thousand years! When you are resurrected, you will obtain a new body. The Bible clearly teaches that you will not be just a spirit floating around—you will have a new physical body that will never age and that has supernatural characteristics. It will be impossible to not welcome the new body God gives you when you suddenly realize how much healthier and more amazing it is than your present one.

HELL

Is there really a place called hell?

MATTHEW 7:13 | *You can enter God's Kingdom only through the narrow gate. The highway to hell is broad, and its gate is wide for the many who choose that way.*

REVELATION 20:15 | *Anyone whose name was not found recorded in the Book of Life was thrown into the lake of fire.*

The greatest misconception about hell is that it doesn't exist. Just as we believe scientists when they tell us there is such a thing as gravity, we should believe God when he tells us there is such a place as hell. Many people ask why a merciful and caring God would send people to such a terrible place. The truth is that God doesn't send anyone to hell; people choose to go there by their own rebellion, and God honors their choice. The Bible is clear: Sin is rebellion against God, and rebels can't live in a kingdom without causing chaos. The only way to avoid hell is to surrender to God and change from a rebel to a servant. He then forgives us and lets us enter and live in his Kingdom forever. At the end of time, each of us will be judged for the choice we've made. Although God desperately wishes that no one should live in hell, he respects us enough to let us choose.

HOLINESS

What does it mean to be holy and to live a holy life?

LEVITICUS 20:26 | *You must be holy because I, the LORD, am holy. I have set you apart from all other people to be my very own.*

ROMANS 12:1 | *Give your bodies to God because of all he has done for you. Let them be a living and holy sacrifice—the kind he will find acceptable.*

1 CORINTHIANS 1:2 | *I am writing to . . . you who have been called by God to be his own holy people. He made you holy by means of Christ Jesus, just as he did for all people everywhere who call on the name of our Lord Jesus Christ.*

1 CORINTHIANS 6:11 | *You were cleansed; you were made holy; you were made right with God.*

Think of holiness as both a journey and a final destination. To be completely holy is to be sinless, pure, and perfect before God. Of course, no one is perfect yet—that is your ultimate goal, your final condition, when you stand before God in heaven. But holiness also means to be different, to be "set apart" by God for a specific purpose. You are to be different from the rest of the world, and your life is a journey toward becoming a little more pure and sinless with each passing day.

EPHESIANS 1:4 | *Even before he made the world, God loved us and chose us in Christ to be holy and without fault in his eyes.*

COLOSSIANS 1:22 | *[God] has reconciled you to himself through the death of Christ in his physical body. As a result, he has brought you into his own presence, and you are holy and blameless as you stand before him without a single fault.*

God does not regard you as righteous because you are sinless, but because Jesus died to take your sins away. No one but Jesus Christ lived a sinless life, but a person who acknowledges Jesus as Lord becomes more holy by sincerely trying to live in obedience to God's Word. Anyone who has asked God to forgive his or her sin can be called holy. In other words, when God forgives you, because of what Christ did on the cross for you he looks at you as though you have not sinned. What an amazing concept that God sent his Son to die for your sins so that he could see only holiness when he looks at you.

In what ways is God holy?

1 SAMUEL 6:20 | *Who is able to stand in the presence of the LORD, this holy God?*

God is completely separate from sin and evil. He is perfect and has no sin in him.

ISAIAH 6:3 | *Holy, holy, holy is the LORD of Heaven's Armies! The whole earth is filled with his glory!*

God is dazzling and glorious in his absolute purity. God's holiness is so glorious that it not only fills heaven but is reflected in nature on earth.

AMOS 4:2 | *The Sovereign LORD has sworn . . . by his holiness.*

When God makes a promise, his holiness ensures that he will always do what he says.

MATTHEW 13:41 | *The Son of Man will send his angels, and they will remove from his Kingdom everything that causes sin and all who do evil.*

God's holiness will not tolerate evil in his eternal Kingdom.

HOLY SPIRIT

Who is the Holy Spirit, and how do I receive him?

LUKE 24:49 | *[Jesus said,] "I will send the Holy Spirit, just as my Father promised. But stay here in the city until the Holy Spirit comes and fills you with power from heaven."*

ACTS 2:1-4 | *On the day of Pentecost all the believers were meeting together in one place. Suddenly, there was a sound from heaven like the roaring of a mighty windstorm, and it filled the house where they were sitting. Then, what looked like flames or tongues of fire appeared and settled on each of them. And everyone present was filled with the Holy Spirit and began speaking in other languages, as the Holy Spirit gave them this ability.*

EPHESIANS 1:14 | *The Spirit is God's guarantee that he will give us the inheritance he promised and that he has purchased us to be his own people. He did this so we would praise and glorify him.*

Who is the Holy Spirit? God is three persons in one—the Father, the Son, and the Holy Spirit. God became a human being in Jesus so that Jesus could die for the sins of the world. Jesus rose from the dead to offer salvation to all people through spiritual rebirth. When Jesus ascended into heaven, his physical presence left the earth, but he promised to send the Holy Spirit so that his spiritual presence would still be among his people. The Holy Spirit became available to all believers first at Pentecost (see Acts 2). Whereas in the Old Testament days the Holy Spirit empowered specific individuals for specific purposes, now all believers have the power of the Holy Spirit available to them.

EPHESIANS 3:16 | *I pray that from [God's] glorious, unlimited resources he will empower you with inner strength through his Spirit.*

The Holy Spirit is the power of God that lives in every believer. When you yield control of your life to the Holy Spirit, he releases his power within you—power to resist temptation, to serve and love God and others even when you are at the end of your rope, to have wisdom in all circumstances, and to persevere in living for God now with the promise of eternal life later.

When do I receive the Holy Spirit?

EPHESIANS 1:13-14 | *When you believed in Christ, he identified you as his own by giving you the Holy Spirit, whom he promised long ago. The Spirit is God's guarantee that he will give us the inheritance he promised and that he has purchased us to be his own people. He did this so we would praise and glorify him.*

God gave you the Holy Spirit when you first believed in Jesus Christ. In fact, it was through the promptings of the Holy Spirit that you were able to believe in Jesus.

ACTS 2:16-18 | *[Peter said,] "What you see was predicted long ago by the prophet Joel: 'In the last days,' God says, 'I will pour out my Spirit upon all people. Your sons and daughters will prophesy. Your young men will see visions, and your old men will dream dreams. In those days I will pour out my Spirit even on my servants—men and women alike—and they will prophesy.'"*

The gift of the Holy Spirit was promised long ago but was not made available to all believers until Jesus Christ was resurrected and ascended into heaven. Peter's preaching at Pentecost marked the dramatic outpouring of the Spirit, fulfilling the prophecies of old.

LUKE 11:11-13 | *If your children ask for a fish, do you give them a snake instead? Or if they ask for an egg, do you give them a scorpion? Of course not! So if you sinful people know how to give good gifts to your children, how much more will your heavenly Father give the Holy Spirit to those who ask him.*

Though the Holy Spirit lives within you, you pray expectantly that God will release more and more of the Spirit's power in your life. In a way, the Holy Spirit is like electricity—only when you are plugged in and you turn on the switch does the power flow.

LUKE 12:11-12 | *When you are brought to trial in the synagogues and before rulers and authorities, don't worry about how to defend yourself or what to say, for the Holy Spirit will teach you at that time what needs to be said.*

ACTS 1:8 | *[Jesus said,] "You will receive power when the Holy Spirit comes upon you. And you will be my witnesses, telling people about me everywhere—in Jerusalem, throughout Judea, in Samaria, and to the ends of the earth."*

The Lord gives you an extra measure of the Holy Spirit whenever you need special power and courage to witness for him.

How does the Holy Spirit help me?

1 CORINTHIANS 2:12 | *We have received God's Spirit (not the world's spirit), so we can know the wonderful things God has freely given us.*

The Holy Spirit helps you understand the deep truths of God.

GALATIANS 5:16-17 | *Let the Holy Spirit guide your lives. Then you won't be doing what your sinful nature craves. The sinful nature wants to do evil, which is just the opposite of what the Spirit wants. And the Spirit gives us desires that are the opposite of what the sinful nature desires.*

The Holy Spirit convicts you of sin and shows you right from wrong, good from bad, and God's way versus the way of the world. The Holy Spirit shows you how to live a life that pleases God.

ROMANS 8:26-27 | *The Holy Spirit helps us in our weakness. For example, we don't know what God wants us to pray for. But the Holy Spirit prays for us with groanings that cannot be expressed in words. And the Father who knows all hearts knows what the Spirit is saying, for the Spirit pleads for us believers in harmony with God's own will.*

The Holy Spirit helps you pray. You can take great comfort and have confidence in the fact that your prayers—as inadequate as they often are—are heard, understood, and responded to through the loving intercession of the Holy Spirit.

1 CORINTHIANS 6:19 | *Don't you realize that your body is the temple of the Holy Spirit, who lives in you and was given to you by God?*

EPHESIANS 5:18-20 | *Be filled with the Holy Spirit, singing psalms and hymns and spiritual songs among yourselves, and making music to the Lord in your hearts. And give thanks for everything to God the Father in the name of our Lord Jesus Christ.*

The Holy Spirit gives you the power and desire to resist temptations that would dishonor God or hurt you. He also makes your worship of God more joyful and meaningful.

ROMANS 8:16 | *His Spirit joins with our spirit to affirm that we are God's children.*

The Holy Spirit fills you with the assurance that you are a child of God, saved from sin.

HONESTY

Why is honesty so essential?

LUKE 16:10 | *If you are faithful in little things, you will be faithful in large ones. But if you are dishonest in little things, you won't be honest with greater responsibilities.*

Your honesty matters greatly to God because it reveals your character. If you can't be trusted to be honest in a small matter, who can trust you to be honest in a big matter? That's why honesty is the test for responsibility. When you have built your life with bricks of honesty, you have a strong foundation to act with integrity when great challenges and responsibilities come your way. When your life is governed by God's standards of fairness and justice, you'll be ready to carry out God's purposes for your life, and others will trust and follow you.

HOPE

How do I trust God as my hope?

PSALM 94:19 | *When doubts filled my mind, your comfort gave me renewed hope and cheer.*

Hope, by definition, is expecting something that has not yet occurred. Faith and patience keep hope alive. Have faith that God will do what he has promised, and be patient while he does it in his own time and in his own way. You can be absolutely sure that he is already acting on your behalf, because God is trustworthy.

How can I cultivate greater hope?

PROVERBS 10:28 | *The hopes of the godly result in happiness, but the expectations of the wicked come to nothing.*

1 PETER 1:3-4, 6 | *God raised Jesus Christ from the dead. Now we live with great expectation, and we have a priceless inheritance—an inheritance that is kept in heaven for you, pure and undefiled, beyond the reach of change and decay. . . . There is*

wonderful joy ahead, even though you have to endure many trials for a little while.

What could make you more joyful than knowing you will live forever in a perfect world? No matter how hopeless things seem now, joy can burn in your heart as you focus on eternity, for in Jesus you have ultimate hope. People who don't know Jesus Christ have nothing but a hopeless view of what happens after death. But those who know him have been promised a joyful, eternal future in heaven, and that knowledge brings hope.

Why is hope such an important part of love?

1 CORINTHIANS 13:7 | *Love never gives up, never loses faith, is always hopeful, and endures through every circumstance.*

One characteristic of authentic love is hope. God, in his great love, never gets tired of giving you second chances. He always thinks the best of you, always encourages you to be the best you can be, always patiently waits for you to love him and others more and more. And when you've forgotten or neglected him, he yearns for the slightest possibility that you will return to restore your relationship with him. He promises that if you learn to truly love, you will have this same kind of hope.

HUMILITY

How does humility help me serve God better?

PHILIPPIANS 2:5-8 | *You must have the same attitude that Christ Jesus had. Though he was God, he did not think of equality with God as something to cling to. Instead, he gave up his divine privileges; he took the humble position of a slave and was born as a human being. When he appeared in human form, he humbled himself in obedience to God and died a criminal's death on a cross.*

Humility is the pathway to service. True humility results from understanding who you are and who God is. Humility allows you to serve wherever God places you and to do whatever God asks of you. Patients who regain health through a physician's care are more humble because they realize their vulnerability. Likewise, you are humbled when you realize that God healed your soul and you realize your complete dependence on him. When you do, you're happy to serve your Lord in any way he asks.

What is the value of a humble spirit?

MATTHEW 18:4 | *Anyone who becomes as humble as this little child is the greatest in the Kingdom of Heaven.*

Humility is true strength, for its effects reach into the Kingdom of Heaven. Pride is true weakness, for it reaches no further than your own ego.

JAMES 4:6-10 | *[God] gives us even more grace to stand against such evil desires. As the Scriptures say, "God opposes the proud but favors the humble." So humble yourselves before God. Resist the devil, and he will flee from you. Come close to God, and God will come close to you. Wash your hands, you sinners; purify your hearts, for your loyalty is divided between God and the world. Let there be tears for what you have done. Let there be sorrow and deep grief. Let there be sadness instead of laughter, and gloom instead of joy. Humble yourselves before the Lord, and he will lift you up in honor.*

Humility is essential to recognizing the sin in your life. Whereas pride gives the devil the key to your heart, humility gives God the key. In place of pride is the humility that comes from godly sorrow for sin. Openly admit that you need God, and seek his forgiveness. No proud person can do this.

INFLUENCE

What does it mean to be "in" the world and not "of" it?

2 KINGS 17:8 | *They had followed the practices of the pagan nations the LORD had driven from the land ahead of them, as well as the practices the kings of Israel had introduced.*

The people of Israel were given laws and rules to set them apart from the surrounding pagan cultures. But instead of influencing the cultures around them for God, they were influenced by them to break God's rules. As a Christian, you should be aware of your culture and the practices that are not godly. Determine to stand up and be a godly influence on your culture, rather than let it influence you.

PSALM 8:6-9 | *You gave them charge of everything you made, putting all things under their authority— the flocks and the herds and all the wild animals, the birds in the sky, the fish in the sea, and everything that swims the ocean currents. O LORD, our Lord, your majestic name fills the earth!*

1 CORINTHIANS 3:22-23 | *Everything belongs to you, and you belong to Christ, and Christ belongs to God.*

People who don't believe in Jesus Christ are "of" the world and become chained to the things their culture says offer security and happiness. They are of the world because they have no eternal purpose and see no future after this life, so their culture is all they've got. They live only off the messages and values taught by their culture because that is all they know.

As believers in Christ, we live in our culture with everyone else, but we don't need to be enslaved by it because we are able to see that it offers a false promise of security. That is why believers in Christ should not be of our culture, for we know that life on earth is just a tiny part of eternal living. We are not enslaved by our culture because it is our belief in Christ, not our possessions, that gives eternal value to our actions. We are free to use all that God has given us to influence the culture and to invest our lives for the future, not for the present.

What can I do to have a greater influence?

1 CHRONICLES 4:9-10 | *There was a man named Jabez who was more honorable than any of his brothers. . . . He was the one who prayed to the God of Israel, "Oh, that you would bless me and expand my territory! Please be with me in all that I do, and keep me from all trouble and pain!" And God granted him his request.*

GALATIANS 6:8-10 | *Those who live to please the Spirit will harvest everlasting life from the Spirit. So let's not get tired of doing what is good. At just the right time we will reap a harvest of blessing if we don't give up. Therefore, whenever we have the opportunity, we should do good to everyone—especially to those in the family of faith.*

Begin by reaching out and loving those God has placed in your sphere of influence. The power of God can bring the most unlikely people together as friends to become a team with great impact. And pray, as Jabez did, that God would expand your territory. You will be surprised at what God can and will do through you if you are willing.

INJUSTICE

What should I do about injustice in my community and in the world?

HEBREWS 13:3 | *Remember those in prison, as if you were there yourself. Remember also those being mistreated, as if you felt their pain in your own bodies.*

Step up to the plate—don't ignore those being treated unjustly. Be an advocate for people who are mistreated or who are suffering for whatever reasons, and your heart will turn more and more toward helping them.

PSALM 82:3 | *Give justice to the poor and the orphan; uphold the rights of the oppressed and the destitute.*

PROVERBS 31:8-9 | *Speak up for those who cannot speak for themselves; ensure justice for those being crushed. Yes, speak up for the poor and helpless, and see that they get justice.*

Speak out on behalf of those who are oppressed. It is amazing how speaking up—in love—often makes a difference.

JOB 29:16 | *I was a father to the poor and assisted strangers who needed help.*

PROVERBS 24:11-12 | *Rescue those who are unjustly sentenced to die; save them as they stagger to their death. Don't excuse yourself by saying, "Look, we didn't know." For God understands all hearts, and he sees you. He who guards your soul knows you knew. He will repay all people as their actions deserve.*

ISAIAH 1:17 | *Learn to do good. Seek justice. Help the oppressed. Defend the cause of orphans. Fight for the rights of widows.*

Act on your convictions and do something, anything, to help those in need.

PSALM 58:10 | *The godly will rejoice when they see injustice avenged.*

1 CORINTHIANS 13:6 | *[Love] does not rejoice about injustice but rejoices whenever the truth wins out.*

Rejoice with others when justice prevails. Injustice requires mourning. Justice requires celebration.

INNER CONFLICT

What is this conflict I seem to have within myself?

ROMANS 7:15, 19, 22-24 | *I don't really understand myself, for I want to do what is right, but I don't do it. Instead, I do what I hate. . . . I don't want to do what is wrong, but I do it anyway. . . . I love God's law with all my heart. But there is another power within me that is at war with my mind. This power makes me a slave to the sin that is still within me. Oh, what a miserable person I am! Who will free me from this life that is dominated by sin and death?*

Christians struggle daily with inner conflict. You have given your life to Christ, but the old human nature still exists. You know the attitudes and behavior that Christ desires, but you also know how hard it is to live that way all the time. You wrestle with how easy it seems to sin, or to do what you want at the expense of others, or to think more of yourself than of others, or to give in to temptation. There is a constant conflict going on within you because you don't want to be this way. Ironically, good can come from this kind of conflict. It shows that your conscience is still sensitive to sin and that you truly desire to do what is right. If there were no such struggle going on within you, it could indicate that you were too accepting of sin in your life. Turn your struggles over to God each time you are tempted, and let the Holy Spirit help you win the conflicts.

INSIGNIFICANCE

My life feels so small. How can I make it count for God?

ZECHARIAH 4:10 | *Do not despise these small beginnings, for the LORD rejoices to see the work begin.*

ACTS 20:24 | *My life is worth nothing to me unless I use it for finishing the work assigned me by the Lord Jesus—the work of telling others the Good News about the wonderful grace of God.*

Deep within your heart—within every human heart—is a yearning for significance, for your life to count, to make a difference, to be worth something. Perhaps you, like most people, struggle with feeling insignificant—feeling that you're not doing anything truly important or making a difference. Or perhaps you spend more time paralyzed by what you cannot do than acting on what you can do; your inabilities overshadow your abilities. It seems that everywhere you look, you see others who are more successful, more gifted, more this, more that. It is no wonder you feel insignificant! But one of the great lessons of the Bible is that the heroes of the faith—people like Moses, Gideon, Esther, and Peter—were very ordinary people who learned that their significance came not from what *they* could accomplish with their abilities, but from what *God* could accomplish through their abilities. Significance comes first from knowing you are a unique creation of almighty God, who has given you specific abilities he wants to use for a bigger purpose. When you use your God-given abilities to accomplish his work, your life becomes significant, both now and for eternity.

INTEGRITY

What is integrity?

PSALM 18:24-25 | *The LORD rewarded me for doing right. He has seen my innocence. To the faithful you show yourself faithful; to those with integrity you show integrity.*

Integrity is the quality of living up to your moral values, a meshing of your heart and your actions; it is essentially the unity between your character and the character of

God. This union results in your character becoming more and more like his. Integrity is a process. Just as pure gold is the result of a refining process that purifies the metal and tests it with fire, the process of living with integrity is refining. You are tested daily to see how pure you are within. If, in testing you, God finds your heart and actions becoming increasingly pure, then you are living more and more in union with God and are striving for integrity.

JESUS CHRIST

Who is Jesus Christ?

JOHN 3:16-17 | *God loved the world so much that he gave his one and only Son, so that everyone who believes in him will not perish but have eternal life. God sent his Son into the world not to judge the world, but to save the world through him.*

ROMANS 3:23-25 | *Everyone has sinned; we all fall short of God's glorious standard. Yet God, with undeserved kindness, declares that we are righteous. He did this through Christ Jesus when he freed us from the penalty for our sins. For God presented Jesus as the sacrifice for sin. People are made right with God when they believe that Jesus sacrificed his life, shedding his blood.*

ROMANS 5:8-11 | *God showed his great love for us by sending Christ to die for us while we were still sinners. And since we have been made right in God's sight by the blood of Christ, he will certainly save us from God's condemnation. For since our friendship with God was restored by the death of his Son while we were still his enemies, we will certainly be saved through the life of his Son. So now we can rejoice in our wonderful new relationship with God because our Lord Jesus Christ has made us friends of God.*

ROMANS 8:34 | *Christ Jesus died for us and was raised to life for us, and he is sitting in the place of honor at God's right hand, pleading for us.*

ROMANS 10:9 | *If you confess with your mouth that Jesus is Lord and believe in your heart that God raised him from the dead, you will be saved.*

PHILIPPIANS 2:6-11 | *Though [Jesus] was God, he did not think of equality with God as something to cling to. Instead, he gave up his divine privileges; he took the humble position of a slave and was born as a human being. When he appeared in human form, he humbled himself in obedience to God and died a criminal's death on a cross. Therefore, God elevated him to the place of highest honor and gave him the name above all other names, that at the name of Jesus every knee should bow, in heaven and on earth and under the earth, and every tongue confess that Jesus Christ is Lord, to the glory of God the Father.*

Jesus Christ is the Son of God, the Messiah who was promised by God. He was fully God and fully human. He lived a sinless life so that when he died on the cross he could take the punishment that you deserved for your sins. Then he rose from the dead, proving that he has power even over death and assuring you that if you

believe in him as Lord you will not suffer eternal death
but will be raised to everlasting life. You will live in
heaven with him forever.

Why did Jesus have to die on the cross?

ROMANS 6:6 | *We know that our old sinful selves were crucified
with Christ so that sin might lose its power in our lives. We are
no longer slaves to sin.*

1 CORINTHIANS 1:30 | *Christ made us right with God; he made us
pure and holy, and he freed us from sin.*

TITUS 2:14 | *[Jesus Christ] gave his life to free us from every kind
of sin, to cleanse us, and to make us his very own people, totally
committed to doing good deeds.*

All people are guilty of the crime of sin against God. Sin
is unholy and a rebellion against a holy God, and rebels
can't be allowed in God's Kingdom because they cause
conflict and chaos. Jesus actually paid the consequences
for your crime, so you are no longer a rebel to God. But
you must believe and accept what he did. Then you will
be welcomed into heaven to live with him forever. Faith in
Jesus removes your sin and makes you holy and acceptable
in God's sight—Christ's death on the cross was the only
way for you to be saved from the power of sin's control
over your life here on earth. You no longer need to be a
slave to your sin if you accept what Jesus did for you and
ask him for forgiveness and guidance in your life. Jesus
did not die on the cross only to help you get into heaven
but also to help you live a life of purpose and be free from
letting sin control you.

JOY

What is joy?

PSALM 16:11 | *You will show me the way of life, granting me the joy of your presence and the pleasures of living with you forever.*

PSALM 68:3 | *Let the godly rejoice. Let them be glad in God's presence. Let them be filled with joy.*

ROMANS 5:1-2 | *Since we have been made right in God's sight by faith, we have peace with God because of what Jesus Christ our Lord has done for us. Because of our faith, Christ has brought us into this place of undeserved privilege where we now stand, and we confidently and joyfully look forward to sharing God's glory.*

ROMANS 5:11 | *We can rejoice in our wonderful new relationship with God because our Lord Jesus Christ has made us friends of God.*

Joy is the celebration of walking with God. It is an inner happiness that lasts despite the circumstances around you because it is based on a relationship with Jesus Christ. It is peace with God. It is realizing how privileged you are to have your sins forgiven, to be friends with God Almighty, and to be certain you will live forever with him in heaven. It is experiencing the dramatic change that occurs in your life when you allow the Holy Spirit to control your heart and your thoughts.

If God promises me joy, does that mean I'll always be happy? Am I missing joy if I don't feel happy?

PHILIPPIANS 4:4 | *Always be full of joy in the Lord. I say it again—rejoice!*

PHILIPPIANS 4:11-12 | *I have learned how to be content with whatever I have. . . . I have learned the secret of living in every situation.*

JAMES 1:2 | *When troubles come your way, consider it an opportunity for great joy.*

God does not promise constant happiness; in fact, the Bible assures you that problems will come your way because of the kind of world in which you live. But God does promise lasting joy for all who loyally follow him. This kind of joy stays with you despite your problems because you know that God is with you to help you through them and that he will one day take them all away. You can have lasting joy even when you have temporary unhappiness. This is what it means to live with an eternal perspective.

JUDGMENT

Will God really judge me for my sins?

ROMANS 5:9-10 | *Since we have been made right in God's sight by the blood of Christ, he will certainly save us from God's condemnation. For since our friendship with God was restored by the death of his Son while we were still his enemies, we will certainly be saved through the life of his Son.*

One of the hardest things to accept, yet one of the most important, is that you don't make the rules for how life really works. God does. His rules say that sin deserves eternal death and that everyone has sinned. Your salvation is based on the fact that Jesus Christ stood in your place for the judgment you deserve for your sin and on God's promise that he no longer looks at you as an enemy but as a friend—even as his own child. However, your *activities* will be judged, to see if you did them to please God or to please yourself.

JUSTICE

Does God care about justice?

ISAIAH 56:1-2 | *This is what the LORD says: "Be just and fair to all. Do what is right and good, for I am coming soon to rescue you and to display my righteousness among you. Blessed are all those who are careful to do this."*

When you are burdened with trouble, it is tempting to think that God is not fair or just. How can he allow a Christian to suffer when so many unbelievers down the street are prospering? But God has made it clear in the Bible that justice and fairness, while always right, will often be perverted in this life by selfish people. The Bible also makes it clear that justice will not be twisted forever. True justice will one day prevail for all who follow God. Knowing that promise keeps you fighting for justice now while resting in the fact that everything will be set right in the future—forever.

LIMITATIONS

What does God think when he looks at me with all my faults and limitations?

JUDGES 6:11-12, 15 | *Gideon son of Joash was threshing wheat at the bottom of a winepress to hide the grain from the Midianites. The angel of the LORD appeared to him and said, "Mighty hero, the LORD is with you!" . . . "But Lord," Gideon replied, "how can I rescue Israel? My clan is the weakest in the whole tribe of Manasseh, and I am the least in my entire family!"*

The angel of the Lord greeted Gideon by calling him a "mighty hero." Was God talking to the right person? This was Gideon, the man hiding in a winepress from his enemies, the man who claimed he was "the least" of his entire family. Yet God called him a mighty hero. God's message to Gideon—and to you—is clear: You are more than what you think you are. God calls out the best in you. He sees more in you than you see in yourself. You may look at your limitations, but God looks at your potential. If you want to change your perspective, learn to see life from God's viewpoint. He doesn't put nearly as many limitations on you as you do. He sees you for who he intended you to be, who he created you to be. How encouraging that the creator and sustainer of the universe looks at you for who you can become rather than for who you are. What are you afraid of? In what areas is God calling you out from hiding?

EPHESIANS 3:20 | *All glory to God, who is able, through his mighty power at work within us, to accomplish infinitely more than we might ask or think.*

In God's unlimited knowledge, he created you with limitations, not to discourage you but to help you realize your need for him. It is in your weakness that God's strength shines. And when you accomplish something great despite your limitations, it is obvious that God was working through you and that he deserves the credit. Jesus says that what is humanly impossible is possible with God. The next time life makes you aware of your limitations, instead of being discouraged, see it as an opportunity for God's power to defy your limitations, and enjoy the divine moment of having him work through you to accomplish more than you could have ever dreamed.

LISTENING

How can I better listen to God?

PROVERBS 8:32 | *Listen to me, for all who follow my ways are joyful.*

Just as a piano is tuned against a standard tuning fork, so you become in tune with God only when you compare yourself against his standards for living found in the Bible. As God communicates to you through his Word, you will begin to "hear," or discern, just what he wants of you. As your "spiritual hearing" is fine tuned, you will become a good listener and will be able to hear clearly when God calls you to a certain task that he has reserved just for you. And there is nothing that brings greater joy than to be in tune with God.

PSALM 5:3 | *Each morning I bring my requests to you and wait expectantly.*

PSALM 46:10 | *Be still, and know that I am God!*

PROVERBS 1:23 | *Come and listen to my counsel. I'll share my heart with you and make you wise.*

LUKE 8:18 | *Pay attention to how you hear. To those who listen to my teaching, more understanding will be given. But for those who are not listening, even what they think they understand will be taken away from them.*

God can speak to you in many ways, but you must be paying attention. One way to do this is to schedule a special quiet time with God each day where you are quiet before him, waiting expectantly for him to answer. God often speaks to you in these quiet times as you pray and read his Word. God can also speak to you at unexpected times through the words of a close friend, through the instruction of a wise teacher, through a beautiful sunset or a song that moves you. Always pay attention to the many ways in which God speaks to you, and make sure to carve out time when you can more easily hear him. Don't miss an opportunity for a lesson from the Master Teacher. The more you listen to God, the more you will hear him.

LOVE

How can I love God with all my heart, soul, and strength?

DEUTERONOMY 6:5 | *You must love the LORD your God with all your heart, all your soul, and all your strength.*

PSALM 91:14-16 | *The LORD says, "I will rescue those who love me. I will protect those who trust in my name. When they call on me, I will answer; I will be with them in trouble. I will rescue and honor them. I will reward them with a long life and give them my salvation."*

PSALM 116:1 | *I love the LORD because he hears my voice and my prayer for mercy.*

JOHN 13:35 | *[Jesus said,] "Your love for one another will prove to the world that you are my disciples."*

1 JOHN 4:12 | *If we love each other, God lives in us, and his love is brought to full expression in us.*

In modern culture, love is often defined in romantic or sentimental terms. According to the Bible, love is indeed a feeling, but it is also more than feelings. The Bible teaches that love is a commitment that both protects and produces passionate feelings. As a commitment, love is not dependent on warm feelings, but rather on a consistent and courageous decision to extend yourself for the well-being of another. Just as loving feelings can produce commitment, so commitment can produce loving feelings. Jesus became the perfect demonstration of God's unconditional love for you by his commitment in love to lay down his life for your benefit. When you love God with all your heart, soul, and strength, you are making a consistent and courageous decision to develop a relationship with the creator of the universe, who loved you first and who daily pursues you with that love.

How can I show my love for God?

MICAH 6:8 | *The LORD has told you what is good, and this is what he requires of you: to do what is right, to love mercy, and to walk humbly with your God.*

JOHN 14:15 | *[Jesus said,] "If you love me, obey my commandments."*

JOHN 15:10-11 | *[Jesus said,] "When you obey my commandments, you remain in my love. . . . I have told you these things so that you will be filled with my joy. Yes, your joy will overflow!"*

Obedience is an important way to express your love for God. This should not be confused with earning God's love by doing good works. You obey God because you are *already* loved, not in order to be loved. As you obey, you will experience increasing joy because you will see God at work in your life every day. What small step of obedience can you take right now?

What if I just don't like some other Christians? Some can be pretty annoying.

ROMANS 12:9-10, 16 | *Don't just pretend to love others. Really love them. . . . Take delight in honoring each other. . . . Live in harmony with each other. Don't be too proud to enjoy the company of ordinary people. And don't think you know it all!*

PHILIPPIANS 2:3 | *Be humble, thinking of others as better than yourselves.*

1 PETER 2:21 | *God called you to do good, even if it means suffering, just as Christ suffered for you. He is your example, and you must follow in his steps.*

It's easy to like people who are likable, but we model more of God's love when we serve those who are annoying. You'll never find a perfect church, and you'll never find a perfect group of people—even among Christians—so don't go looking for that. Instead, seek God's guidance as to where you should be, and then take joy in reaching out and loving those God has placed in your sphere of influence. You may be surprised at how the power of God can bring the most unlikely people together as friends. When you reach out to others in love, your heart is also changed.

1 CORINTHIANS 13:4-7, 13 | *Love is patient and kind. Love is not jealous or boastful or proud or rude. It does not demand its own way. It is not irritable, and it keeps no record of being wronged. It does not rejoice about injustice but rejoices whenever the truth wins out. Love never gives up, never loses faith, is always hopeful, and endures through every circumstance. . . . Three things will last forever—faith, hope, and love—and the greatest of these is love.*

People are more confused about love than ever. Love is the greatest of all human qualities, and it is an attribute of God himself. Love involves unselfish service to others, which is the evidence that you truly care even if others don't care in return. Faith is the foundation and content of God's message; hope is the attitude and focus; love is the action. Love proves that your faith and your hope are genuine.

1 PETER 4:8 | *Most important of all, continue to show deep love for each other, for love covers a multitude of sins.*

What does it mean that "love covers a multitude of sins"? Love—true love—is unconditional. No matter what others have done to you, regardless of how their mistakes have hurt you, you love in return. When people sin against you or hurt you deeply, you don't retaliate. Then the cycle of sin and hurt stops. Only love can do that.

LOVE OF GOD

How can I know that God really loves me?

1 JOHN 4:9-10 | *God showed how much he loved us by sending his one and only Son into the world so that we might have eternal life through him. This is real love—not that we loved God, but that he loved us and sent his Son as a sacrifice to take away our sins.*

Love is willing to sacrifice for the good of others, even unto death. You can know for certain of God's great love for you because he allowed his Son to die in your place, to take the punishment for your sin so that you can be free from eternal judgment. Think of it: He sent his Son to *die* for you so that you could live forever with him. No wonder John wrote, "This is real love."

LYING

Why does the Bible speak out so strongly about lying?

1 PETER 3:10 | *The Scriptures say, "If you want to enjoy life and see many happy days, keep your tongue from speaking evil and your lips from telling lies."*

Lying is deceiving someone. It can be blatant—"I didn't touch that cake" (as you swallow the last bite)—or it can be subtle, such as telling only part of the truth when it benefits you to do so. Lying is selfish and self-serving, for it always attempts to hide and deceive, to own something you have not earned, or to leave an impression you do not deserve. To fall short of truth, in any way, is to lie. You cannot follow the God of truth while you consistently tell lies— even "small" ones. Lying shatters trust, and trust is the key to strong relationships. That is why the Bible promises that a happy life is an honest life.

MATURITY

How do I begin to mature in my faith?

COLOSSIANS 2:7 | *Let your roots grow down into him, and let your lives be built on him. Then your faith will grow strong in the truth you were taught, and you will overflow with thankfulness.*

Reading the Bible and praying to God are the first and most important steps toward Christian maturity. When your faith is rooted in the Word of God, you will continually be nourished as you soak up the wisdom you read in its pages. When you faithfully spend time talking with God, you are connecting with the source of wisdom. No wonder you will mature as you stay close to him. Seek wisdom from the source so you will grow stronger and more mature in your faith.

EXODUS 24:13 | *Moses and his assistant Joshua set out, and Moses climbed up the mountain of God.*

TITUS 2:1-8 | *As for you, Titus, . . . teach the older men to exercise self-control, to be worthy of respect, and to live wisely. . . . Similarly, teach the older women to live in a way that honors God. . . . These older women must train the younger women to love their husbands and their children, to live wisely and be pure, to work in their homes, to do good, and to be submissive to their husbands. Then they will not bring shame on the word of God. In the same way, encourage the young men to live wisely. And you yourself must be an example to them by doing good works of every kind. Let everything you do reflect the integrity and seriousness of your teaching. Teach the truth so that your teaching can't be criticized.*

Good spiritual mentors can help you grow and mature in your faith, as well as in everyday life. Look for people who are several stages ahead of you in life, who have weathered many experiences, and who exemplify godliness. Ask them to help you learn how to become a mature Christian and a mature person.

MEANING/SIGNIFICANCE

How does being a Christian bring more meaning to life? Does my life really matter to God?

PSALM 16:11 | *You will show me the way of life, granting me the joy of your presence and the pleasures of living with you forever.*

PSALM 39:4 | *LORD, remind me how brief my time on earth will be. Remind me that my days are numbered—how fleeting my life is.*

ISAIAH 43:7 | *Bring all who claim me as their God, for I have made them for my glory. It was I who created them.*

A primary cause of despair is the conviction that life is ultimately meaningless. Why keep trying if it really doesn't matter? Conversely, a sense that your life has meaning gives you energy, purpose, and resilience, even in the middle of problems. God, as your Creator, gives you value, and he promises that your life matters to him. You are made in his image, and his very breath gives you life. You were created to know God and to enjoy fellowship with him. What could be more meaningful than a relationship with God, your Creator?

PSALM 40:8 | *I take joy in doing your will, my God, for your instructions are written on my heart.*

ACTS 20:24 | *My life is worth nothing to me unless I use it for finishing the work assigned me by the Lord Jesus.*

You don't need to do earthshaking things in order to have a meaningful life. Your life has meaning when you do the work that God has given you to do. Whether you are doing homework, hanging out with friends, running a company, or evangelizing the world, when you do it to please God, your life has meaning because you are sharing the love of God with everyone in your circle of influence.

EXODUS 3:11 | *Moses protested to God, "Who am I to appear before Pharaoh? Who am I to lead the people of Israel out of Egypt?"*

Moses offered every excuse in the book for why he was too insignificant to do God's work, but God saw great potential in him. Don't prevent God from working through you to accomplish great things. God can and wants to transform your insecurities into great accomplishments, because for every person God designed a purpose for living.

ESTHER 4:13-14 | *Mordecai sent this [message] to Esther: "Don't think for a moment that because you're in the palace you will escape when all other Jews are killed. If you keep quiet at a time like this, deliverance and relief for the Jews will arise from some other place, but you and your relatives will die. Who knows if perhaps you were made queen for just such a time as this?"*

Esther was only a young girl, but God brought her to a position of great influence in order to save the Jewish people. God uses even those with insignificant beginnings to fulfill his purpose and plan and to bring significant results.

MERCY

What is God's mercy? Why do I need it?

PSALM 103:8-10 | *The LORD is compassionate and merciful, slow to get angry and filled with unfailing love. He will not constantly accuse us, nor remain angry forever. He does not punish us for all our sins; he does not deal harshly with us, as we deserve.*

LAMENTATIONS 3:22-23 | *The faithful love of the LORD never ends! His mercies never cease. Great is his faithfulness; his mercies begin afresh each morning.*

1 PETER 1:3 | *All praise to God, the Father of our Lord Jesus Christ. It is by his great mercy that we have been born again.*

Mercy is undeserved favor—compassion poured out on people who deserve less but receive more, who should expect anger but receive grace. God's mercy goes one step further. God's mercy is more than exemption from the punishment you deserve for your sins. It is receiving an undeserved gift: salvation from eternal death, including life forever in heaven. Even when you don't deserve mercy, God still extends it to you. Your rebellion against God deserves his punishment, but instead he offers you forgiveness and eternal life. Even more, God's mercies never end. He never stops giving you his undivided attention and his faithful presence, as well as spiritual gifts, provision for your needs, and hope for your future—all undeserved and yet lavishly poured out in your life. It is by his mercies that your very life is sustained. It is a divine moment when you realize your very breath is a merciful gift from an all-loving God.

MONEY

What is a proper perspective toward money?

MATTHEW 6:21 | *[Jesus said,] "Wherever your treasure is, there the desires of your heart will also be."*

The Bible mentions many wealthy people who loved God while saying nothing negative about the *amount* of wealth they owned (examples are Abraham, David, Joseph of Arimathea, Lydia). Scripture doesn't focus on how much money you can or cannot have, but rather on what you do with what you have. Jesus made one thing clear: Wherever your money goes, your heart will follow after it. So work hard and succeed without guilt, but make sure to work just as hard at finding ways to please God with your money.

PSALM 23:1 | *The LORD is my shepherd; I have all that I need.*

ECCLESIASTES 5:10 | *Those who love money will never have enough. How meaningless to think that wealth brings true happiness!*

Money can cultivate a dangerous craving—the more you have, the more you want. It is a vicious cycle that never has a satisfactory conclusion. Keep reminding yourself that God must be first in your life and that money cannot satisfy your deepest needs.

PSALM 119:36 | *Give me an eagerness for your laws rather than a love for money!*

HEBREWS 13:5 | *Don't love money; be satisfied with what you have. For God has said, "I will never fail you. I will never abandon you."*

Money is not the root of all evil; the love of money is!

DEUTERONOMY 8:17-18 | *[God] did all this so you would never say to yourself, "I have achieved this wealth with my own strength and energy." Remember the LORD your God. He is the one who gives you power to be successful, in order to fulfill the covenant he confirmed to your ancestors with an oath.*

Wealth and prosperity should not be your goals, nor are they definitive signs of God's blessing—many who lack material possessions are rich in other ways. Prosperity, when given by God, is to be received with gratitude and humility, and it is to be shared with generosity and by gracious hospitality.

PROVERBS 19:1 | *Better to be poor and honest than to be dishonest and a fool.*

MARK 8:36 | *What do you benefit if you gain the whole world but lose your own soul?*

No amount of money is worth deception or dishonesty. Taking advantage of others to make money is stealing. Those who do this lose far more than they gain.

MOTIVES

How can I have purer motives?

1 CORINTHIANS 4:4 | *My conscience is clear, but that doesn't prove I'm right. It is the Lord himself who will examine me and decide.*

Remember that God alone knows your heart. Ask him to reveal to you any area in which your motives are less than pure.

PSALM 19:14 | *May the words of my mouth and the meditation of my heart be pleasing to you, O LORD, my rock and my redeemer.*

Ask God to change the way you think by changing your heart.

1 CHRONICLES 28:9 | *Learn to know . . . God . . . intimately. Worship and serve him with your whole heart and a willing mind. For the LORD sees every heart and knows every plan and thought. If you seek him, you will find him.*

Your attitude toward God is a good indicator of your motives toward others. If you are halfhearted in the way you approach your relationship with God, chances are your motives toward others may be more halfhearted and self-centered than they should be.

PSALM 26:2 | *Put me on trial, LORD, and cross-examine me. Test my motives and my heart.*

2 THESSALONIANS 1:11 | *We keep on praying for you, asking our God to enable you to live a life worthy of his call. May he give*

you the power to accomplish all the good things your faith prompts you to do.

Welcome it when God tests your motives. This gives you an opportunity to grow.

PROVERBS 21:2 | *People may be right in their own eyes, but the LORD examines their heart.*

Before you do something, remember that God is as interested in your motives as he is in your actions.

What are some wrong motives?

JAMES 3:15 | *Jealousy and selfishness are not God's kind of wisdom.*

If you let jealousy motivate you, your actions will be selfish and will hurt others.

GENESIS 27:11-12 | *"Look," Jacob replied to Rebekah, "my brother, Esau, is a hairy man, and my skin is smooth. What if my father touches me? He'll see that I'm trying to trick him, and then he'll curse me instead of blessing me."*

Fear of getting caught is not a good motive because it means you're up to something wrong.

1 SAMUEL 18:17 | *Saul thought, "I'll send [David] out against the Philistines and let them kill him rather than doing it myself."*

PROVERBS 10:11 | *The words of the godly are a life-giving fountain; the words of the wicked conceal violent intentions.*

If you are motivated to harm someone, you are being overcome by evil desires.

EZEKIEL 33:31 | *[The Lord said to Ezekiel,] "My people come pretending to be sincere and sit before you. They listen to your words, but they have no intention of doing what you say."*

Pretending to be close to God is displeasing to him; he knows if your motives are not sincere and you are just trying to put on a good front.

MATTHEW 6:1 | *Watch out! Don't do your good deeds publicly, to be admired by others, for you will lose the reward from your Father in heaven.*

You shouldn't do good in order to be admired by people— you should do it to please God alone.

MATTHEW 22:16-18 | *[The Pharisees] sent some of their disciples, along with the supporters of Herod, to meet with [Jesus]. "Teacher," they said, "we know how honest you are. You teach the way of God truthfully. You are impartial and don't play favorites. Now tell us what you think about this: Is it right to pay taxes to Caesar or not?" But Jesus knew their evil motives. "You hypocrites!" he said. "Why are you trying to trap me?"*

Appearing sincere while being motivated by a desire to trap others and make them look bad is wrong.

What are some right motives?

EXODUS 25:2 | *Tell the people of Israel to bring me their sacred offerings. Accept the contributions from all whose hearts are moved to offer them.*

ISAIAH 11:3 | *He will delight in obeying the LORD.*

To serve God simply because you want to.

HEBREWS 11:4 | *It was by faith that Abel brought a more acceptable offering to God than Cain did. Abel's offering gave evidence that he was a righteous man, and God showed his approval of his gifts. Although Abel is long dead, he still speaks to us by his example of faith.*

To follow the example of a godly person because you want to live a more godly life.

2 CHRONICLES 1:10 | *[Solomon said,] "Give me the wisdom and knowledge to lead them properly, for who could possibly govern this great people of yours?"*

To grow in wisdom and knowledge in order to serve God more effectively.

JOHN 21:17 | *"Simon son of John, do you love me?" Peter was hurt that Jesus asked the question a third time. He said, "Lord, you know everything. You know that I love you." Jesus said, "Then feed my sheep."*

To help others out of love for Jesus, not out of a desire for personal praise or as a way to impress God.

GALATIANS 6:4 | *Pay careful attention to your own work, for then you will get the satisfaction of a job well done, and you won't need to compare yourself to anyone else.*

To do the right thing because it is right, not because it will benefit you or impress others.

NEEDS

What—and whom—do I really need?

MATTHEW 5:3 | *God blesses those who . . . realize their need for him, for the Kingdom of Heaven is theirs.*

HEBREWS 7:26 | *He is the kind of high priest we need because he is holy and blameless, unstained by sin. He has been set apart from sinners and has been given the highest place of honor in heaven.*

You need God—his love, his mercy, his presence, his salvation, his forgiveness, and his promise of eternal life.

LUKE 17:5 | *The apostles said to the Lord, "Show us how to increase our faith."*

EPHESIANS 6:16 | *Hold up the shield of faith to stop the fiery arrows of the devil.*

You need faith to stand firm in the face of temptation.

JAMES 1:5 | *If you need wisdom, ask our generous God, and he will give it to you. He will not rebuke you for asking.*

You need God's wisdom and guidance so that you know where to go in life's journey and how to do what is right, helpful, and pleasing to him along the way.

2 CORINTHIANS 12:9 | *Each time [the Lord] said, "My grace is all you need. My power works best in weakness." So now I am glad to boast about my weaknesses, so that the power of Christ can work through me.*

You need God's strength to help you in times of weakness.

LUKE 18:1 | *One day Jesus told his disciples a story to show that they should always pray and never give up.*

You need to pray often to keep you in constant communication with God.

PSALM 119:75 | *I know, O LORD, that your regulations are fair; you disciplined me because I needed it.*

You need the Lord's discipline to keep you following his ways.

ROMANS 12:4-5, 13 | *Just as our bodies have many parts and each part has a special function, so it is with Christ's body. We are many parts of one body, and we all belong to each other. . . . When God's people are in need, be ready to help them.*

You need other Christians, encouraging you and serving with you.

What do I need to do?

LUKE 18:1 | *One day Jesus told his disciples a story to show that they should always pray and never give up.*

You need to pray, to stay in constant communication with God.

2 CORINTHIANS 12:9 | *[God] said, "My grace is all you need. My power works best in weakness." So now I am glad to boast about my weaknesses, so that the power of Christ can work through me.*

You need to depend on God's strength to help you in times of weakness.

JAMES 1:5 | *If you need wisdom, ask our generous God, and he will give it to you. He will not rebuke you for asking.*

You need to ask God for wisdom and guidance. He has promised to give it to you freely just for the asking.

Does God really care about my daily needs?

ISAIAH 46:4 | *I will be your God throughout your lifetime— until your hair is white with age. I made you, and I will care for you. I will carry you along and save you.*

2 CORINTHIANS 9:8-9 | *God will generously provide all you need. Then you will always have everything you need and plenty left over to share with others. As the Scriptures say, "They share freely and give generously to the poor. Their good deeds will be remembered forever."*

PHILIPPIANS 4:19 | *This same God who takes care of me will supply all your needs from his glorious riches, which have been given to us in Christ Jesus.*

When you learn to distinguish between your wants and your needs, you will begin to understand how God provides and you will realize how much he truly cares for you. God doesn't promise to give you a lot of possessions, but he does promise to help you possess the character traits that reflect his nature so that you can accomplish his plan for you. He doesn't promise to preserve your physical life, but he does promise to keep your soul for all eternity if you've pledged your allegiance to him.

NEIGHBORS

What does it mean to love my neighbor?

LEVITICUS 19:18 | *Love your neighbor as yourself. I am the LORD.*

MATTHEW 22:37-39 | *Jesus [said], "'You must love the LORD your God with all your heart, all your soul, and all your mind.' This is the first and greatest commandment. A second is equally important: 'Love your neighbor as yourself.'"*

ROMANS 13:8 | *If you love your neighbor, you will fulfill the requirements of God's law.*

Jesus taught that to love your neighbor as yourself is the second-greatest commandment. Why do the Old Testament writers and Jesus say to love your neighbor as yourself? Because God knows that your first instinct is to take care of yourself. But if you can train yourself to give the needs of others equal priority with your own, then you will have learned what love is all about. If you truly love others the way God intended, you will naturally carry out all God's other instructions for service. Love directed inward has nowhere else to go. Love directed outward can change the world, one person at a time.

OBEDIENCE

Is obedience to God really necessary, since I am saved by faith?

DEUTERONOMY 6:18 | *Do what is right and good in the LORD's sight, so all will go well with you.*

PSALM 84:11 | *The LORD God is our sun and our shield. He gives us grace and glory. The LORD will withhold no good thing from those who do what is right.*

God's call for your obedience is based on his own commitment to your well-being—since God is the Creator of life, he knows how life is supposed to work. His commandments are not burdensome obligations but pathways to a joyful, meaningful, and satisfying life. Even though they are sometimes difficult or don't make sense from a human perspective, obedience to him will always bring blessing, joy, and peace. It demonstrates your willingness and trust to follow through on what God says is best for you and is the visible expression of your love for God.

LEVITICUS 9:6 | *Moses said, "This is what the LORD has commanded you to do so that the glory of the LORD may appear to you."*

Obedience to God brings you into fellowship with him, allowing you to find out what his will is for you.

What happens when I obey God?

JEREMIAH 7:23 | *Obey me, and I will be your God, and you will be my people. Do everything as I say, and all will be well!*

Obedience is defined as "being submissive to an authority." Ironically, obedience to God's ways actually frees you to enjoy life as he originally created it, keeping you from becoming entangled or enslaved to the sinful things that distract or hurt you. It protects you from the evil that God knows is there, leads you on right paths where you will find blessing, and directs you into service that will please him.

How can I possibly obey all God's commandments consistently?

DEUTERONOMY 8:1 | *Be careful to obey all the commands I am giving you today.*

GALATIANS 5:17 | *The sinful nature wants to do evil, which is just the opposite of what the Spirit wants. And the Spirit gives us desires that are the opposite of what the sinful nature desires. These two forces are constantly fighting each other, so you are not free to carry out your good intentions.*

The rule for perfect living is to obey all God's commandments. But no one is perfect. That's why Jesus Christ died and rose again—to make it possible to forgive your

sins. The key, therefore, is to consistently *try* to obey
God's commandments, realizing that you will fail sometimes. At the point of your failure, go to Jesus and ask his
forgiveness.

DEUTERONOMY 30:15-16 | *Now listen! Today I am giving you a choice
between life and death, between prosperity and disaster. For I
command you this day to love the LORD your God and to keep his
commands, decrees, and regulations by walking in his ways. If you
do this, you will live . . . and the LORD your God will bless you.*

Commit yourself to make the little daily choices to serve
God. Serving God with your life begins with small decisions to serve him. The more you commit to serving God
in the little things, the more you will want to obey him.
Obedience is a life commitment to daily godly choices.

Is following God hard?

1 CHRONICLES 28:20 | *David [said], "Be strong and courageous,
and do the work. Don't be afraid or discouraged, for the LORD
God, my God, is with you. He will not fail you or forsake you.
He will see to it that all the work . . . is finished correctly."*

JAMES 1:2-4 | *When troubles come your way, consider it an
opportunity for great joy. For you know that when your faith is
tested, your endurance has a chance to grow. So let it grow, for
when your endurance is fully developed, you will be perfect and
complete, needing nothing.*

Just because you are following God in something doesn't
make it easy. In fact, the more important a task is, the more
Satan will put up roadblocks. If you know God is leading you
in a certain direction, don't give up just because the going

gets tough. If anything, that should tell you that you are headed in the right direction. Keep moving forward boldly with your eyes fixed on God. Your faith will be strengthened as you obey him in your life and in your daily choices.

OPPORTUNITIES

How do I know if an opportunity is from God?

1 THESSALONIANS 5:17 | *Never stop praying.*

Stay close to God through prayer and ask for his guidance.

JOSHUA 1:7 | *Be careful to obey all the instructions Moses gave you. Do not deviate from them, turning either to the right or to the left. Then you will be successful in everything you do.*

PSALM 119:105 | *Your word is a lamp to guide my feet and a light for my path.*

Though the Bible will not always speak directly about a particular opportunity, any opportunity that contradicts God's Word or leads you away from its principles is not from God.

PROVERBS 15:22 | *Plans go wrong for lack of advice; many advisers bring success.*

Seek the wisdom of trustworthy, mature Christians.

DEUTERONOMY 1:28-30 | *Where can we go? Our brothers have demoralized us with their report. They tell us, "The people of the land are taller and more powerful than we are, and their towns are large, with walls rising high into the sky! We even saw giants there.*" . . . *But [Moses said], "Don't be shocked or afraid of them! The* LORD *your God is going ahead of you.*"

Don't let fear and doubt cause you to miss God's opportunities. God often sends opportunities that require faith and courage to teach you to trust him.

MATTHEW 25:21 | *Well done, my good and faithful servant. You have been faithful in handling this small amount, so now I will give you many more responsibilities.*

God presents everyone with the ability and the opportunity to invest for the good and the growth of his Kingdom.

OPPOSITION

What does the Bible mean when it says I will face opposition for following Jesus?

JOHN 15:18-19 | *If the world hates you, remember that it hated me first. The world would love you as one of its own if you belonged to it, but you are no longer part of the world. I chose you to come out of the world, so it hates you.*

ROMANS 8:31 | *If God is for us, who can ever be against us?*

Evil can't stand the sight of Jesus and can't bear to even hear his name. So if you are living in a way that others can clearly see Jesus in you, there is bad news and good news. The bad news is that you will face opposition and even persecution for your faith. Satan opposes Jesus, so if you are living for Jesus, you share a common enemy in Satan. The good news is that with Jesus on your side, you cannot lose the battle for your soul. Even if the whole world is against you, God is for you and promises to give you spiritual victories in this life and ultimate victory for eternity.

OVERCOMING

Will God help me escape life's troubles?

JOB 17:9 | *The righteous keep moving forward, and those with clean hands become stronger and stronger.*

LUKE 4:1-2 | *Jesus, full of the Holy Spirit, returned from the Jordan River. He was led by the Spirit in the wilderness, where he was tempted by the devil for forty days. Jesus ate nothing all that time and became very hungry.*

Overwhelmed, defeated, powerless, out of control—you may sometimes feel like there's no way to overcome your circumstances or struggles. In life you will be confronted by immense obstacles and seemingly invincible opponents. But take heart! The ability to overcome is the birthright of believers. And God has given you his presence, the Holy Spirit, to help you triumph over the obstacles and temptations in your life. God's presence doesn't mean the absence of struggle. Being filled with the Holy Spirit did not prevent Jesus from being tempted, but it helped him overcome temptation. As long as you live on this earth, you will never be free from trouble, but you can have the power to prevail over it. Only when you desire and allow the Holy Spirit to work in you will he help you overcome.

When you begin to see the obstacles in your life as opportunities for God to show his power, they will not seem so overwhelming. The very hardships and weaknesses that frighten you may be the tools God wants to use to help you prevail.

PASSION

Why am I not always on fire for God?

1 KINGS 11:1-3 | *King Solomon loved many foreign women. . . . He married women from Moab, Ammon, Edom, Sidon. . . . The LORD had clearly instructed the people, . . . "You must not marry them, because they will turn your hearts to their gods." Yet Solomon insisted on loving them anyway. . . . And in fact, they did turn his heart away from the LORD.*

When sin takes a foothold in your life, it always leads you away from God and substitutes an apathetic attitude toward him. Satan will use all his power to keep you from being excited about following God. While no one can avoid sin entirely, it is possible to recognize when sin starts to control you. It is at this point that you need to run back to God so that you can once again be passionate about serving him.

GENESIS 3:6 | *The woman was convinced. She saw that the tree was beautiful and its fruit looked delicious, and she wanted the wisdom it would give her. So she took some of the fruit and ate it. Then she gave some to her husband, who was with her, and he ate it, too.*

1 CORINTHIANS 10:13 | *The temptations in your life are no different from what others experience. And God is faithful. He will not allow the temptation to be more than you can stand. When you are tempted, he will show you a way out so that you can endure.*

1 JOHN 4:4 | *The Spirit who lives in you is greater than the spirit who lives in the world.*

Temptation takes your focus off God and makes thinking about something else more exciting. When this happens, it's not that you intend to move away from God, but something else has suddenly captured your attention! If what you're excited about is not what God wants for you, your passion for God will quickly die. But don't worry, for God will provide you a way out of temptation if you ask him to. You will then be able to see why following God and his way is more exciting than giving in to the temptation to sin. Try following God the next time temptation comes. The feeling of purpose and satisfaction will restore your passion for serving God.

COLOSSIANS 1:22-23 | *You are holy and blameless as you stand before [God] without a single fault. But you must continue to believe this truth and stand firmly in it. Don't drift away from the assurance you received when you heard the Good News.*

HEBREWS 2:1 | *We must listen very carefully to the truth we have heard, or we may drift away from it.*

REVELATION 2:4 | *[God said,] "I have this complaint against you. You don't love me or each other as you did at first!"*

Like all relationships, your relationship with God takes effort and energy. God continues to be fully committed to you. In order for your relationship to continue to be exciting, you must be fully committed to him—diligent in your efforts to know him better. Four things can really make a difference: Studying God's Word, communicating with him in prayer, maintaining a thankful heart, and serving others will fight off feelings of apathy toward God and renew your focus on his purpose for your life and the blessings he has given you and will give you in the future.

PEACE

Why should I pursue peace?

PSALM 34:14-15 I *Turn away from evil and do good. Search for peace, and work to maintain it. The eyes of the LORD watch over those who do right; his ears are open to their cries for help.*

We are called to work and pray for peace in the world. This will happen as more people make peace with God—and truly understand what that means. When you pursue peace with others, God says he is more actively involved in your life. Why? Because people who pursue peace are pursuing his agenda. With God's help and your commitment to peace, you can make a difference.

PERSEVERANCE

How do I develop the perseverance to get through tough times?

2 CORINTHIANS 1:8-9 | *We think you ought to know . . . about the trouble we went through in the province of Asia. We were crushed and overwhelmed beyond our ability to endure, and we thought we would never live through it. In fact, we expected to die. But as a result, we stopped relying on ourselves and learned to rely only on God, who raises the dead.*

PHILIPPIANS 1:6 | *God, who began the good work within you, will continue his work until it is finally finished on the day when Christ Jesus returns.*

COLOSSIANS 1:11 | *We . . . pray that you will be strengthened with all his glorious power so you will have all the endurance and patience you need. May you be filled with joy.*

Perseverance has been well defined as "courage stretched out." Although God sometimes delivers you from difficult or painful circumstances, he often calls you to a courageous and enduring faithfulness in the middle of trials. Perseverance, according to the Bible, is not only enduring difficult situations but overcoming them with obedience, hope, and joy. If you don't learn to persevere through your struggles, you will simply develop the habit of giving up. But when you persevere until you come out on the other side, you grow stronger in faith, you see the benefits of obedience to God, and you develop greater confidence that when problems strike again you can get through them.

If I am saved by grace and not by works, why is perseverance so important?

JAMES 5:11 | *We give great honor to those who endure under suffering.*

Perseverance in good works does not produce salvation. Rather, perseverance in doing good is evidence that your faith in God is real.

2 PETER 1:5-6 | *Supplement your faith with a generous provision of . . . patient endurance, and patient endurance with godliness.*

Through patient perseverance, you become more like Jesus. Becoming more like Jesus is important not only for you but also for others, to show them what being a Christian is all about.

JAMES 1:3 | *You know that when your faith is tested, your endurance has a chance to grow.*

Perseverance turns adversity into maturity. Suffering for the sake of suffering has no point. But adversity that leads to maturity and growth is productive and life changing.

PLANNING

Doesn't planning ahead conflict with trusting God to lead me? If it doesn't, how should I make my plans?

1 CHRONICLES 28:12, 19 | *David also gave Solomon all the plans he had in mind for the courtyards of the LORD's Temple, the outside rooms, the treasuries, and the rooms for the gifts dedicated to the*

LORD. . . . *"Every part of this plan," David told Solomon, "was given to me in writing from the hand of the LORD."*

Rather than conflicting with trust in God, planning helps you put your faith in God into action. God will lead you, but it is your responsibility to recognize his lead, make a plan, and follow through. God's work doesn't happen simply by chance; he needs capable people who are willing to plan ahead and do the work.

PROVERBS 22:3 | *A prudent person foresees danger and takes precautions. The simpleton goes blindly on and suffers the consequences.*

Planning prepares you for life. A person who doesn't plan will always be caught off guard by difficult circumstances, but the person who plans ahead will be able to face the difficulties of life with confidence. The most important plans you can make will involve how you are preparing yourself for eternity. The way you live now has everything to do with where and how you will live in the afterlife.

PSALM 138:8 | *The LORD will work out his plans for my life.*

PROVERBS 19:21 | *You can make many plans, but the LORD's purpose will prevail.*

Planning demonstrates your desire to use your time wisely and makes you a good steward of the time and resources God has given you. So make your plans, but hold them loosely because you can be assured that God will give you new marching orders from time to time. You must be ready and willing to adjust because his plans for you will lead you in the direction you want to be going.

ACTS 18:21 | *[Paul] said, "I will come back later, God willing." Then he set sail from Ephesus.*

Follow God's revealed will when you make your plans. If his will is not clear in a specific matter, remember that he has made his will clear in general matters of right and wrong, good and bad, helpful and harmful. So you can move ahead with your plans as long as you are confident they do not go against God's Word. As you do, don't be surprised if God intervenes to alter them.

PLEASURE

Some seem to think that pleasure and the Christian life don't mix—is that true?

PSALM 1:1-2 | *Oh, the joys of those who do not follow the advice of the wicked . . . but they delight in the law of the LORD.*

PSALM 112:1 | *Praise the LORD! How joyful are those who fear the LORD and delight in obeying his commands.*

Some of the greatest pleasures come from pleasing God and experiencing the peace and joy that are the rewards of a faithful life of purpose.

1 TIMOTHY 4:4-5 | *Since everything God created is good, we should not reject any of it but receive it with thanks. For we know it is made acceptable by the word of God and prayer.*

God intends for you to enjoy the life he gave you and the good things he created for all people.

NEHEMIAH 8:10 | *Nehemiah continued, "Go and celebrate with a feast of rich foods and sweet drinks, and share gifts of food with people who have nothing prepared. This is a sacred day before our Lord. Don't be dejected and sad, for the joy of the LORD is your strength!"*

It is good to enjoy occasions of celebrating God's goodness and love.

PSALM 16:11 | *You will show me the way of life, granting me the joy of your presence and the pleasures of living with you forever.*

JOHN 10:10 | *[Jesus said,] "The thief's purpose is to steal and kill and destroy. My purpose is to give them a rich and satisfying life."*

God created you with the capacity to find pleasure in your relationship with him. It is amazing the things you discover about yourself and the awesome emotions you feel when you are in prayer with God. There are many times that you will feel God's presence, and that feeling is indescribable.

PSALM 127:4-5 | *Children born to a young man are like arrows in a warrior's hands. How joyful is the man whose quiver is full of them!*

God wants you to enjoy the blessing of your family.

SONG OF SONGS 7:6 | *Oh, how beautiful you are! How pleasing, my love, how full of delights!*

Marriage was God's idea, as well as the pleasures of intimacy that go along with that unique relationship.

JOHN 4:34 | *Jesus [said]: "My nourishment comes from doing the will of God, who sent me, and from finishing his work."*

The best kind of pleasure is delighting in doing what God wants. This brings us great satisfaction and a sense of fulfillment. As children of God, we long to please our Father, just as earthly children love to please their parents.

ECCLESIASTES 2:1, 10-11 | *[Solomon] said to [himself], "Come on, let's try pleasure. Let's look for the 'good things' in life."... Anything I wanted, I would take. I denied myself no pleasure. ... But as I looked at everything I had worked so hard to accomplish, it was all so meaningless—like chasing the wind. There was nothing really worthwhile anywhere.*

Not all pleasure is good, and sometimes you pursue the wrong pleasures, those that ultimately harm you or that bring no meaning or purpose to your life. In pursuing the wrong pleasures, your life will eventually seem meaningless when you discover you've been wasting your time chasing after the wrong things.

POWER

As a new Christian, what kind of power can I really have?

EPHESIANS 1:19-20 | *I . . . pray that you will understand the incredible greatness of God's power for us who believe him. This is the same mighty power that raised Christ from the dead and seated him in the place of honor at God's right hand in the heavenly realms.*

EPHESIANS 6:10 | *Be strong in the Lord and in his mighty power.*

2 THESSALONIANS 1:11 | *We keep on praying for you, asking our God to enable you to live a life worthy of his call. May he give*

*you the power to accomplish all the good things your faith
prompts you to do.*

God, who created the world and who defeats Satan, offers
his power to you. If you believe that God sent Jesus Christ
to save you from sin and if you ask him to forgive your sin
and remove it, he will replace your sin-filled heart with the
power to do good, to accomplish great things, and to resist
the forces of evil. But you can use God's power only for
godly purposes.

2 CORINTHIANS 12:9 | *[God] said, "My grace is all you need. My
power works best in weakness."*

The more you recognize your weaknesses and limitations,
the more you understand God's power at work in you.
Strength can make you proud and self-sufficient. You don't
believe that you need to rely much on God or others when
you are very good at something or have great authority.
That is why God often works through your weaknesses—if
you let him—because then there is no doubt that it is by his
power and not your own that the task is getting done.

2 CHRONICLES 16:9 | *The eyes of the LORD search the whole earth in
order to strengthen those whose hearts are fully committed to him.*

JOHN 15:5 | *[Jesus said,] "Yes, I am the vine; you are the
branches. Those who remain in me, and I in them, will
produce much fruit. For apart from me you can do nothing."*

God gives his strength to those who are fully committed
to him. Just as a branch needs to be connected to a tree to
grow and thrive, you need to be connected to him to grow
and thrive spiritually.

PRAISE

How can I be inspired to praise God?

1 CHRONICLES 16:25-26 | *Great is the LORD! He is most worthy of praise! He is to be feared above all gods. The gods of other nations are mere idols, but the LORD made the heavens!*

LUKE 19:36-38 | *As [Jesus] rode along, the crowds spread out their garments on the road ahead of him. . . . All of his followers began to shout and sing as they walked along, praising God for all the wonderful miracles they had seen. "Blessings on the King who comes in the name of the LORD! Peace in heaven, and glory in highest heaven!"*

2 THESSALONIANS 1:10 | *When he comes on that day, he will receive glory from his holy people—praise from all who believe. And this includes you, for you believed what we told you about him.*

It is not unusual for observers to burst into spontaneous applause or cheers when a celebrity enters a room. This is a natural response to the presence of a person of power, position, or accomplishment. Likewise, when you enter the presence of God through worship, your natural response should be praise and adoration. The Bible teaches that God is the creator of the universe—he fashioned the heavens, placed the planets and stars in motion, carved out the canyons and valleys and mountains, and breathed life into every human being. Furthermore, he desires a personal relationship with you and even provides a way for you to live in heaven with him forever. As the creator and the sustainer of life, he alone is worthy of your highest praise. Perhaps the best way to realize the awesome power and presence of God is to consider his greatness in comparison to your mortality and weakness. As you consider his unlimited and unconditional love for you personally, despite your limitations, you will begin to find yourself naturally responding to him with more adoration, joy, and praise.

PRAYER

What is prayer?

2 CHRONICLES 7:14 | *[The Lord said,] "If my people who are called by my name will humble themselves and pray and seek my face and turn from their wicked ways, I will hear from heaven."*

PSALM 5:1 | *O LORD, hear me as I pray.*

Prayer is conversation with God. It is simply talking to him, telling him your thoughts and feelings, praising him, thanking him, confessing sin, asking for his help and advice, and listening for his answers. The essence of prayer is humbly entering the very presence of almighty God.

PSALM 38:18 | *I confess my sins; I am deeply sorry for what I have done.*

1 JOHN 1:9 | *If we confess our sins to him, he is faithful and just to forgive us our sins and to cleanse us.*

Prayer often begins with a confession of sin. It is through confession that you demonstrate the humility necessary for open lines of communication with the almighty, holy God.

1 SAMUEL 14:36 | *The priest said, "Let's ask God first."*

2 SAMUEL 5:19 | *David asked the LORD, "Should I go out to fight the Philistines?"*

Prayer is asking God for guidance, then waiting for his direction and leading.

MARK 1:35 | *Before daybreak the next morning, Jesus got up and went out to an isolated place to pray.*

Prayer is an expression of an intimate relationship with your heavenly Father, who makes his own love and resources available to you. Just as you enjoy being with people you love, you will enjoy spending time with God the more you get to know him and understand just how much he loves you.

1 SAMUEL 3:10 | *The LORD came and called as before, "Samuel! Samuel!" And Samuel replied, "Speak, your servant is listening."*

Good conversation also includes listening, so make time for God to speak to you. When you listen to God, he will make his wisdom and plan known to you.

PSALM 8:9 | *O LORD, our Lord, your majestic name fills the earth!*

PSALM 9:1-2 | *I will praise you, LORD, with all my heart; I will tell of all the marvelous things you have done. I will be filled with joy because of you. I will sing praises to your name, O Most High.*

Through prayer, you praise your mighty God.

Why is prayer important?

PSALM 145:18 | *The LORD is close to all who call on him, yes, to all who call on him in truth.*

MATTHEW 7:7-11 | *Keep on asking, and you will receive what you ask for. Keep on seeking, and you will find. Keep on knocking, and the door will be opened to you. For everyone who asks, receives. Everyone who seeks, finds. And to everyone who knocks, the door will be opened. You parents—if your children ask for a loaf of bread, do you give them a stone instead? Or if they ask for a fish, do you give them a snake? Of course not! So if you sinful people know how to give good gifts to your children, how much more will your heavenly Father give good gifts to those who ask him.*

There's more to prayer than just getting an answer to a question or a solution for a problem. God often does more in your heart through the act of prayer than he does in actually answering your prayer. As you persist in conversation with God, you will receive important things such as the power and desire to obey him, the strength to overcome evil with good, the supernatural ability to love and forgive, the character to persevere in your faith, and the courage to be his witness to those who don't know him. You can pray confidently for wisdom and guidance in all situations, knowing that you are asking for the very things God most longs to give.

Does God always answer prayer?

PSALM 116:1 | *I love the LORD because he hears my voice and my prayer for mercy.*

2 CORINTHIANS 12:8-9 | *Three different times [Paul] begged the Lord to take [the thorn in his flesh] away. Each time he said, . . . "My power works best in weakness."*

1 PETER 3:12 | *The eyes of the Lord watch over those who do right, and his ears are open to their prayers.*

God listens carefully to every prayer and answers it. His answer may be *yes, no,* or *wait.* Doesn't any loving parent give all three of these responses to a child at different times? God's answering yes to every request would spoil you and be dangerous to your well-being. Answering no to every request would be vindictive, stingy, and damaging to your spirit. Answering wait to every prayer would be frustrating. God always answers, but his answers are based on what he knows is best for you. When you don't get the answer you want, don't interpret it as silence from God but as a signal that he is pointing you in a specific direction. Your spiritual maturity will grow as you seek to understand that God's answer is in your best interest.

Does prayer—whether others are praying for me or I am praying for them—really make a difference?

2 CORINTHIANS 1:11 | *[Paul said,] "You are helping us by praying for us. Then many people will give thanks because God has graciously answered so many prayers for our safety."*

JAMES 5:16 | *The earnest prayer of a righteous person has great power and produces wonderful results.*

Paul was convinced that the Corinthians' prayers were vitally connected to his deliverance by God. Intercession is the practice of praying for the needs of others. It is easy to become discouraged if you think there is nothing anyone can do for you—or nothing that you can do to help someone you care about. But in fact, the most important thing you can do for others, and that others can do for you, is to pray. In ways beyond human understanding, intercessory prayer is a channel for the love and power of God, as well as creating a deep bond of fellowship between human beings. Thus intercession is a vital source of hope.

ACTS 12:5-9 | *While Peter was in prison, the church prayed very earnestly for him. The night before Peter was to be placed on trial, he was asleep, fastened with two chains between two soldiers. . . . Suddenly, there was a bright light in the cell, and an angel of the Lord stood before Peter. The angel struck him on the side to awaken him and said, "Quick! Get up!" And the chains fell off his wrists. . . . "Follow me," the angel ordered. So Peter left the cell, following the angel.*

Even as the believers were holding an all-night prayer meeting, God sent an angel to rescue Peter from prison.

How can I grow more confident in my prayer life?

HEBREWS 4:14-16 | *Since we have a great High Priest who has entered heaven, Jesus the Son of God, let us hold firmly to what we believe. This High Priest of ours understands our weaknesses, for he faced all of the same testings we do, yet he did not sin. So let us come boldly to the throne of our gracious God. There we will receive his mercy, and we will find grace to help us when we need it most.*

Don't ever be afraid to talk to God. If you don't talk to him much, you won't get to know him well. When you get to know him, you'll discover he's not a harsh dictator ready to punish you for every fault, but a loving Father wanting to comfort, help, forgive, and bless you. The assurance of God's love gives you courage to come to him with any problem, struggle, or concern. Your prayers are never interruptions to the Lord. When you knock, the door will always open for you to meet with him and to talk as long and as freely as you want.

PRIORITIES

What should be my highest priority?

MARK 12:29-30 | *Jesus [said], "The most important command-ment is this: 'Listen, O Israel! The LORD our God is the one and only LORD. And you must love the LORD your God with all your heart, all your soul, all your mind, and all your strength.'"*

Jesus clearly stated the highest priority for every person: Love God, and do it with all you've got. When you sincerely love God, you will also then love others.

PROTECTION

If God promises to protect me, why do I get hurt?

JOB 36:15 | *By means of their suffering, [God] rescues those who suffer. For he gets their attention through adversity.*

PSALM 22:24 | *[The Lord] has not ignored or belittled the suffer-ing of the needy. He has not turned his back on them, but has listened to their cries for help.*

PSALM 126:5-6 | *Those who plant in tears will harvest with shouts of joy. They weep as they go to plant their seed, but they sing as they return with the harvest.*

Suffering is not a sign that God doesn't care; it is simply a fact of life in this sinful world. If God always took away your suffering, you would not need him or desire heaven. More significantly, you would probably follow God for a magic cure rather than for your need of salvation. Some suffering is by chance, such as that caused by an auto accident or an illness. Some is a consequence of neglect, failure, or sin. Suffering is a universal experience, and God uses it to draw people to him. While the Bible never promises a life free from pain, it does assure you, as a believer, that God is with you in your pain and that all pain will one day be gone forever (see Revelation 21:4).

PSALM 31:19-20 | *How great is the goodness you have stored up for those who fear you. You lavish it on those who come to you for protection. . . . You hide them in the shelter of your presence.*

DANIEL 3:17-18 | *The God whom we serve is able to save us. . . . But even if he doesn't, . . . we will never serve your gods.*

God promises to protect you and keep you safe. But the ultimate fulfillment of this promise is in safeguarding your soul so that your body and soul will live with him in heaven forever. Like Daniel's friends, you must commit yourself, no matter what happens to your earthly body, to loving and obeying God to ensure that your heavenly body will be in the right place in eternity.

JEREMIAH 42:13, 16 | *If you refuse to obey the LORD your God, . . . the very war and famine you fear will catch up to you.*

Jeremiah taught about the relationship between your obedience and the protection of God. Obedience to God will protect you from the consequences of disobedience. For example, obeying God's command not to cheat will protect you from the embarrassment, loss of friendships, fines, and potential jail time that can come from cheating.

PURPOSE

How do I find God's specific purpose for my life?

PSALM 40:8 | *I take joy in doing your will, my God, for your instructions are written on my heart.*

PSALM 57:2 | *I cry out to God Most High, to God who will fulfill his purpose for me.*

JOHN 15:16 | *You didn't choose me. I chose you. I appointed you to go and produce lasting fruit, so that the Father will give you whatever you ask for, using my name.*

ACTS 20:24 | *My life is worth nothing to me unless I use it for finishing the work assigned me by the Lord Jesus.*

ROMANS 12:2 | *Let God transform you into a new person by changing the way you think. Then you will learn to know God's will for you, which is good and pleasing and perfect.*

PHILIPPIANS 3:12 | *I press on to possess that perfection for which Christ Jesus first possessed me.*

Do you keep a "to do" list of things you need to accomplish each day, week, or month? Such lists can help bring some sense of purpose to your life, helping you stay focused and on target. If you could reduce your entire life to a short list of only three or four "big" items you want to do, what would they be? The top item on that list should come very close to identifying the purpose of your life, the passion God created inside you. According to the Bible, your purpose is to be inspired by a vision as to how God can best use you to accomplish his goals. God has a general purpose and a specific purpose for you. Your general purpose is to let the love of Jesus shine through you to make an impact on others. More specifically, God has given you spiritual gifts (see Romans 12:6-8; 1 Corinthians 12:4-11; 1 Peter 4:10-11) and wants you to use them to make a unique contribution in your sphere of influence. The better you fulfill your general purpose, the clearer your specific purpose will become. The ultimate goal in life is not to reach the destinations you want, but to reach the destinations God wants for you. As you passionately pursue your purpose as assigned by God, he promises that your life will have lasting meaning, significance, and eternal results.

DANIEL 1:17 | *God gave these four young men an unusual aptitude for understanding every aspect of literature and wisdom. And God gave Daniel the special ability to interpret the meanings of visions and dreams.*

MATTHEW 25:21 | *Well done, my good and faithful servant. You have been faithful in handling this small amount, so now I will give you many more responsibilities.*

1 CORINTHIANS 12:11 | *It is the one and only Spirit who distributes all these gifts. He alone decides which gift each person should have.*

God has given every individual special aptitudes and abilities. These provide the biggest clue to what God wants you to do. When he calls you to do something unique for him, he will almost always allow you to use your God-given gifts to get the job done. Why would God give you certain talents and spiritual gifts and then not ask you to use them? You may be gifted in the area of cooking, entertaining, managing a business, sewing, handling money, playing an instrument, or some other gift. Develop your special abilities and begin to use them, and you will see what God wants you to do.

RECONCILIATION

What is reconciliation, and why is it important?

2 CORINTHIANS 5:19, 21 | *God was in Christ, reconciling the world to himself, no longer counting people's sins against them. And he gave us this wonderful message of reconciliation. . . . For God made Christ, who never sinned, to be the offering for our sin, so that we could be made right with God through Christ.*

One of the most essential truths taught in the Bible is that you, along with all people, were born with a sinful nature, and sin separates you from God. If you want a personal relationship with him, you must be "reconciled" to him, meaning that damage in the relationship needs to be repaired so that you can be on friendly terms. Reconciliation begins by recognizing that without the work of Jesus Christ on the cross, you cannot approach God. God chose to have his Son, Jesus, take your punishment for your sinful rebellion so you could approach God, no longer considered his enemy but his friend. When you accept God's gift of bridging this gap, you are reconciled to him and can begin a relationship with him. This is the greatest gift ever offered—and the only way to be reconciled to God.

2 CORINTHIANS 5:18-21 | *God has given us this task of reconciling people to him. For God was in Christ, reconciling the world to*

himself, no longer counting people's sins against them. . . . We speak for Christ when we plead, "Come back to God!" For God made Christ, who never sinned, to be the offering for our sin, so that we could be made right with God through Christ.

Reconciliation becomes possible only when someone makes the first move: a hand extended, a phone call, a word spoken in forgiveness. In the same way, the relationship between God and the people he created was broken in the Garden of Eden, when sin caused an uncrossable chasm that separates humans from God, and someone had to make the first move. While it is human beings who need to be reconciled, it is God who made the first move. God extended not just his hand, not just words, but his Son, Jesus Christ, to bridge the chasm between himself and his people.

REPENTANCE

What is repentance?

LUKE 24:47 | *There is forgiveness of sins for all who repent.*

ACTS 2:37-38 | *Peter's words pierced [the people's] hearts, and they said to him and to the other apostles, "Brothers, what should we do?" Peter replied, "Each of you must repent of your sins and turn to God."*

ACTS 3:19 | *Repent of your sins and turn to God, so that your sins may be wiped away.*

Have you ever had the experience of driving a car and suddenly realizing you were going the wrong way on a one-way street? What you do next is very much like the biblical idea of repentance. You make a U-turn and change your direction as fast as you can. Repentance is motivated by the realization that you have taken the wrong way in life. The Bible calls this wrong way "sin." Repentance is admitting your sin and making a commitment, with God's help, to change your life's direction. While not a popular concept these days, repentance is essential because it is the only way to arrive at your desired destination—heaven. Because of repentance, change is possible and you can experience God's fullest blessings, both now and for eternity. Repentance is that divine moment when you decide to move toward God and not away from him. Are you going in the right direction?

MATTHEW 3:2 | *Repent of your sins and turn to God.*

GALATIANS 5:24-25 | *Those who belong to Christ Jesus have nailed the passions and desires of their sinful nature to his cross and crucified them there. Since we are living by the Spirit, let us follow the Spirit's leading in every part of our lives.*

Repentance means turning from a life that is ruled by your sinful nature and turning to God for a new nature, which comes when God's Spirit begins to live in you. When God forgives your sins, you will have a new sense of hope for the future.

LUKE 19:8 | *Zacchaeus stood before the Lord and said, "I will give half my wealth to the poor, Lord, and if I have cheated people on their taxes, I will give them back four times as much!"*

Repentance is made complete by changed behavior, showing others and God that your life is truly different in a positive way.

PSALM 32:3-5 | *When I refused to confess my sin, my body wasted away, and I groaned all day long. Day and night your hand of discipline was heavy on me. My strength evaporated like water in the summer heat. Finally, I confessed all my sins to you and stopped trying to hide my guilt. I said to myself, "I will confess my rebellion to the LORD." And you forgave me!*

ROMANS 10:10 | *It is by believing in your heart that you are made right with God, and it is by confessing with your mouth that you are saved.*

One of the first essential steps to repentance is confession, which means being humbly honest with God about your sins—the ones you know about and the ones you are unaware of—as well as sincerely sorry for them. Confession restores your relationship with God, and this renews your strength and your spirit. When you repent, God removes your guilt, restores your joy, and heals your broken soul. A heart that truly longs for change is necessary in order for repentance to be genuine.

Why does God want me to repent? Why is repentance necessary?

PROVERBS 28:13 | *People who conceal their sins will not prosper, but if they confess and turn from them, they will receive mercy.*

ISAIAH 55:7 | *Let the wicked change their ways and banish the very thought of doing wrong. Let them turn to the LORD that he may have mercy on them. Yes, turn to our God, for he will forgive generously.*

1 TIMOTHY 1:16 | *God had mercy on me so that Christ Jesus could use me as a prime example of his great patience with even the worst sinners. Then others will realize that they, too, can believe in him and receive eternal life.*

Repentance is your only hope of receiving God's mercy. Those who refuse to see and admit their sins can't be forgiven for them, and they have placed themselves outside God's mercy and blessing.

LUKE 24:47 | *There is forgiveness of sins for all who repent.*

ACTS 2:37-38 | *Peter's words pierced their hearts, and they said to him and to the other apostles, "Brothers, what should we do?" Peter replied, "Each of you must repent of your sins and turn to God, and be baptized in the name of Jesus Christ for the forgiveness of your sins. Then you will receive the gift of the Holy Spirit.*

Repentance allows you to receive forgiveness. If you are sincere when you come to God and ask him humbly, he will forgive you, no matter how many times you sin and need to repent.

2 CHRONICLES 30:9 | *The LORD your God is gracious and merciful. If you return to him, he will not continue to turn his face from you.*

MATTHEW 3:2 | *Repent of your sins and turn to God, for the Kingdom of Heaven is near.*

Repentance is necessary for an ongoing relationship with God.

Is repentance a one-time event, or do I need to repent each time I sin?

PSALM 51:17 | *The sacrifice you desire is a broken spirit. You will not reject a broken and repentant heart, O God.*

1 JOHN 1:8-9 | *If we claim we have no sin, we are only fooling ourselves and not living in the truth. But if we confess our sins to him, he is faithful and just to forgive us our sins and to cleanse us from all wickedness.*

While salvation is a one-time event, God is pleased by broken and contrite hearts that are willing to continually confess and repent of sin. Confessing and repenting of sin are daily habits of the person walking in the light of fellowship with God.

REPUTATION

Why should I care what people think of me?

PROVERBS 3:1, 3-4 | *My child, never forget the things I have taught you. Store my commands in your heart. . . . Never let loyalty and kindness leave you! Tie them around your neck as a reminder. Write them deep within your heart. Then you will find favor with both God and people, and you will earn a good reputation.*

2 CORINTHIANS 8:20-21 | *[Paul said,] "We are traveling together to guard against any criticism for the way we are handling this generous gift. We are careful to be honorable before the Lord, but we also want everyone else to see that we are honorable."*

COLOSSIANS 3:23-24 | *Work willingly at whatever you do, as though you were working for the Lord rather than for people. Remember that the Lord will give you an inheritance as your reward, and that the Master you are serving is Christ.*

2 PETER 1:5, 8 | *Supplement your faith with a generous provision of moral excellence. . . . The more you grow like this, the more productive and useful you will be.*

Believe it or not, a good reputation can actually help you and others experience God. First, the reputation you strive to achieve should result from being fully committed to building spiritual character in your life, not building an external image. A reputation built on image without substance eventually becomes a crumbling facade. The key to spiritual strength is building your life to mirror the character of God. Second, integrity produces credibility. Your testimony of faith means nothing if your actions contradict what you say. In fact, others will think you foolish. It is sad how often the message of God is discredited or mocked because of a damaged reputation. A godly reputation, built through integrity and humility, spreads the life-changing message of God and the relevancy of his truth. Your life should be the proof others need to accept God's love. Finally, God cares about your reputation. Having a good and honest reputation has many benefits in this life but also brings rewards for eternity. It is important to work hard, not to please others but to please God. By doing this you also honor his reputation. What matters most is not what others think of you, but what God thinks of you.

RESTORATION

How can I know that I have been restored to fellowship with God?

ROMANS 5:10 | *Since our friendship with God was restored by the death of his Son while we were still his enemies, we will certainly be saved through the life of his Son.*

Sin separates you from God, and as long as you remain separated from him, you cannot experience a relationship with him. Worse yet, separation from God sentences you to eternal death. That is why God sent his Son, Jesus, to die in your place. He took the punishment for your sins so you wouldn't have to, and then he gave you the opportunity to overcome the sinful nature you were born with. When God raised Jesus from the dead, it proved his power over sin and it gives you complete assurance of his promise that you can have eternal life with him. So when you believe that Jesus died for your sins and was raised from the dead, you confess your sins and ask God to forgive you, and you commit yourself to obeying him; you are then restored to fellowship with him both now and forever.

RESURRECTION

How can I have confidence that God will someday resurrect me to life in heaven for eternity?

JOHN 11:25 | *Jesus [said], "I am the resurrection and the life. Anyone who believes in me will live, even after dying."*

1 CORINTHIANS 15:12-14 | *Tell me this—since we preach that Christ rose from the dead, why are some of you saying there will be no resurrection of the dead? For if there is no resurrection of the dead, then Christ has not been raised either. And if Christ has not been raised, then all our preaching is useless, and your faith is useless.*

The guarantee that we will be raised from the dead is that Jesus was. Eyewitness evidence for any historical event is the most reliable, and hundreds of eyewitnesses claimed to have seen Jesus following the Resurrection. The apostles were willing to risk martyrdom for preaching the truth about it, and millions upon millions of changed lives bear witness to the fact that Jesus rose from the dead and is alive today. Because of the Resurrection, we know that Christ's sacrifice on the cross accomplished God's plan—our sins are forgiven and we will live with Jesus in heaven forever. Christianity, at its heart, is not another moral or religious code but resurrection and new life.

What does Jesus' resurrection mean to me?

MATTHEW 28:5-6 | *The angel spoke to the women. "Don't be afraid!" he said. "I know you are looking for Jesus, who was crucified. He isn't here! He is risen from the dead, just as he said would happen. Come, see where his body was lying."*

JOHN 3:16 | *God loved the world so much that he gave his one and only Son, so that everyone who believes in him will not perish but have eternal life.*

1 CORINTHIANS 15:42 | *Our earthly bodies are planted in the ground when we die, but they will be raised to live forever.*

Without the resurrection of Jesus from the dead, there would be no Christianity. The Resurrection is central because it demonstrates God's power over death, thereby assuring you that you will also be resurrected. The power of God that brought Jesus back from the dead will also bring you back to life. Jesus' death was not the end. His resurrection is the beginning of eternal life for all who believe in him.

2 CORINTHIANS 4:14 | *We know that God, who raised the Lord Jesus, will also raise us with Jesus and present us to himself together with you.*

COLOSSIANS 1:22 | *[God] has reconciled you to himself through the death of Christ in his physical body. As a result, he has brought you into his own presence, and you are holy and blameless as you stand before him without a single fault.*

Because of Jesus Christ's life, death, and resurrection—and your faith in him—you stand holy and blameless in God's presence. You can come to him confidently. Jesus died for you and rose again with the promise to be with you.

1 PETER 1:21 | *Through Christ you have come to trust in God. And you have placed your faith and hope in God because he raised Christ from the dead.*

The Lord is your source of hope because his promises are true. You lose hope when you stop believing that. The Resurrection, the greatest event in history, is the foundation of your hope. Jesus promised that he would rise from the dead, and because he did, you can be assured that every promise God makes to you will also come true.

RETURN OF JESUS

How should I prepare for the return of Jesus?

MATTHEW 3:2 | *Repent of your sins and turn to God, for the Kingdom of Heaven is near.*

1 PETER 1:13-15 | *Think clearly and exercise self-control. Look forward to the gracious salvation that will come to you when Jesus Christ is revealed to the world. So you must live as God's obedient children. Don't slip back into your old ways of living to satisfy your own desires. You didn't know any better then. But now you must be holy in everything you do, just as God who chose you is holy.*

Prepare for Jesus' coming by committing your life to obeying his instructions for living and by growing closer in your relationship with him. As you do this, you will grow in holiness and be ready when he returns for you.

MATTHEW 24:14 | *The Good News about the Kingdom will be preached throughout the whole world, so that all nations will hear it; and then the end will come.*

When you take part in proclaiming the good news of salvation, you help prepare others for the return of Jesus. Think of methods to which people will be receptive, such as bringing up the subject to a friend when you are eating or hanging out together. Trying to better understand your friend's views will usually result in his or her wanting to understand yours. Then you will have a chance to explain why you are a Christian.

REWARDS

Shouldn't I be receiving rewards for following Jesus?

MATTHEW 6:20 | *Store your treasures in heaven, where moths and rust cannot destroy, and thieves do not break in and steal.*

1 CORINTHIANS 2:9 | *No eye has seen, no ear has heard, and no mind has imagined what God has prepared for those who love him.*

If those who follow God suffer like everybody else, why bother to live for God? It's true, if the rewards of this earthly life were the only thing to live for, then a "Why bother?" attitude would be understandable. But there are two reasons why this perspective is mistaken. First, when you try to obey God, you put yourself in position to enjoy life the way it is meant to be enjoyed: Your relationships are better, your life has more integrity, and your conscience is clear. Second, this life is not all there is. The Bible is very clear that those who trust Jesus Christ for forgiveness of sin receive the promise of eternal life. Your faithfulness in this life may or may not result in material prosperity, but the rewards in heaven will be more than you could ever imagine.

RISK

Why might I have to take risks to keep growing in my Christian life?

PSALM 37:5 | *Commit everything you do to the LORD. Trust him, and he will help you.*

PSALM 91:5 | *Do not be afraid of the terrors of the night, nor the arrow that flies in the day.*

PROVERBS 22:3 | *A prudent person foresees danger and takes precautions. The simpleton goes blindly on and suffers the consequences.*

ECCLESIASTES 10:9 | *When you work in a quarry, stones might fall and crush you. When you chop wood, there is danger with each stroke of your ax.*

LUKE 6:22 | *What blessings await you when people hate you and exclude you and mock you and curse you as evil because you follow the Son of Man.*

2 TIMOTHY 1:7-8 | *God has not given us a spirit of fear and timidity, but of power. . . . So never be ashamed to tell others about our Lord.*

The Bible says that, in the Christian life, spiritual growth and success occur at some risk. Risk taking is actually necessary if you want to grow in your relationship with God. When he calls you to do something out of your comfort zone, obey at the risk of failing, while trusting him to help you complete what he has asked you to do. Only then will your growth take giant steps.

SACRIFICE

Why should I make a habit of sacrificing for others?

LEVITICUS 1:4 | *The LORD will accept [the animal's] death in your place to purify you, making you right with him.*

ROMANS 8:3 | *The law of Moses was unable to save us because of the weakness of our sinful nature. So God did what the law could not do. He sent his own Son in a body like the bodies we sinners have. And in that body God declared an end to sin's control over us by giving his Son as a sacrifice for our sins.*

HEBREWS 9:22 | *Without the shedding of blood, there is no forgiveness.*

HEBREWS 9:27-28 | *Just as each person is destined to die once and after that comes judgment, so also Christ died once for all time as a sacrifice to take away the sins of many people.*

1 PETER 2:24 | *[Christ] personally carried our sins in his body on the cross so that we can be dead to sin and live for what is right. By his wounds you are healed.*

1 JOHN 4:10 | *This is real love—not that we loved God, but that he loved us and sent his Son as a sacrifice to take away our sins.*

A sacrifice is a kind of substitution. Something is given up in order to obtain something else of greater value. Parents may sacrifice buying a new car to save money for their child's education. A baseball player executes a "sacrifice bunt" to give a teammate an opportunity to score a run. In the Old Testament, a sacrifice was an act of worship in which the blood of an animal was shed as a substitute for the punishment people deserved for their sin. It might seem strange and even barbaric that animals would be sacrificed on an altar. But how much worse if a person had to die instead?

Today we are desensitized to the seriousness of sin. But sin is just as serious to God as it has always been. Sin deserves eternal death because it separates us from God. God is holy; we are not. Holiness and sin cannot co-exist. In Old Testament days, God provided a way for the people's sins to be removed so they could be holy in God's eyes. People brought an animal to the altar, and it would become their "substitute," taking their place on the altar. They symbolically transferred their sins to the animal, allowing them to be pure and holy once again before God. When Jesus died on the cross, he transferred the sins of all humankind onto himself—forever (see Hebrews 9:11-15; 10:11-18). No more sacrifices need to be made. Jesus was the last sacrifice. All you must do now is recognize your sin before God and accept his gift of forgiveness.

Anytime you make a sacrifice by giving something up for someone else, you can be reminded, in some small way, of God's sacrifice, the greatest of all. Out of gratitude that God sacrificed so much for you, you should be willing to follow his example and find ways to sacrifice for others.

SALVATION

What does it mean to be saved?

ROMANS 3:22-25 | *We are made right with God by placing our faith in Jesus Christ. And this is true for everyone who believes, no matter who we are. For everyone has sinned; we all fall short of God's glorious standard. Yet God, with undeserved kindness, declares that we are righteous. He did this through Christ Jesus when he freed us from the penalty for our sins. For God presented Jesus as the sacrifice for sin. People are made right with God when they believe that Jesus sacrificed his life, shedding his blood.*

The scenes are captured by the media many times every year: A man is dramatically rescued from a swollen river, a child is pulled by firefighters from a burning apartment building, a woman is delivered from a would-be assailant by a brave bystander. Each scenario includes a situation of impending peril or destruction, a rescuer or deliverer who intervenes, and a second chance at life for the one saved. Although the word is rarely used in the media, each is a picture of salvation. The Bible teaches that sin threatens you with broken relationships, spiritual death, and judgment. When sin controls you, you are in grave danger. But God, through the death and resurrection of Jesus Christ, has provided a way to rescue you from sin's consequences. He offers you salvation so that you can have a second chance at life; an opportunity to experience a spiritual rebirth into a new and abundant life; and, ultimately, eternal life with him forever.

ACTS 4:12 | *There is salvation in no one else! God has given no other name under heaven by which we must be saved.*

Although it may sound exclusive, the Bible's claim of "one way" to salvation is actually an expression of the grace and kindness of God in letting all people know how to escape eternal judgment. God invites anyone and everyone to come to him.

How can I be saved?

ROMANS 10:13 | *Everyone who calls on the name of the LORD will be saved.*

God's Word promises salvation—a guarantee of an eternal, perfect life in heaven—to those who call on Jesus' name to have their sins forgiven. Call out to him in prayer and tell him that you want him to save you. He promises he will.

JOHN 3:16 | *God loved the world so much that he gave his one and only Son, so that everyone who believes in him will not perish but have eternal life.*

ACTS 16:31 | *Believe in the Lord Jesus and you will be saved.*

ROMANS 3:21-22 | *God has shown us a way to be made right with him. . . . We are made right with God by placing our faith in Jesus Christ. And this is true for everyone who believes, no matter who we are.*

Jesus promises that those who believe in him will be saved. All you have to do is accept what Jesus did for you. God sent Jesus Christ to take your place and to receive the punishment that you deserve for your sins. When you believe that he died to save you from your sins and rose again to give you eternal life, then you are saved.

ROMANS 10:9-10 | *If you confess with your mouth that Jesus is Lord and believe in your heart that God raised him from the dead, you will be saved. For it is by believing in your heart that you are made right with God, and it is by confessing with your mouth that you are saved.*

EPHESIANS 2:8 | *God saved you by his grace when you believed. And you can't take credit for this; it is a gift from God.*

It seems too easy. The greatest gift God could ever offer— life in a perfect world forever—is absolutely free. You just have to accept it by (1) agreeing with God that you have sinned, (2) acknowledging that your sin cuts you off from God, (3) asking Jesus to forgive your sins, and (4) believing that Jesus is Lord over everything and that he is the Son of God. The gift is yours if you will choose to receive it.

ROMANS 11:6 | *It is not by their good works. For in that case, God's grace would not be what it really is—free and undeserved.*

You cannot earn your way to heaven by being good and doing kind deeds. Salvation comes only through faith in Jesus.

Is salvation available to anyone?

LUKE 2:11-12 | *The Savior—yes, the Messiah, the Lord—has been born today in Bethlehem, the city of David! And you will recognize him by this sign: You will find a baby wrapped snugly in strips of cloth, lying in a manger.*

Jesus was born in a humble stable among very ordinary people to demonstrate powerfully that salvation is available to anyone who sincerely seeks him.

HEBREWS 9:27 | *Each person is destined to die once and after that comes judgment.*

REVELATION 20:12 | *I saw the dead, both great and small, standing before God's throne. And the books were opened, including the Book of Life. And the dead were judged according to what they had done, as recorded in the books.*

Salvation is available to all, but a time will come when it will be too late to receive it.

SATISFACTION

Why can't I ever feel satisfied with my life?

PSALM 107:9 | *[The Lord] satisfies the thirsty and fills the hungry with good things.*

ECCLESIASTES 1:8 | *No matter how much we see, we are never satisfied. No matter how much we hear, we are not content.*

ISAIAH 55:2-3 | *Why spend your money on food that does not give you strength? . . . Listen to me, and you will eat what is good. . . . Listen, and you will find life.*

EZEKIEL 3:1-3, 10 | *The voice said to me, "Son of man, eat what I am giving you—eat this scroll! Then go and give its message to the people of Israel." So I opened my mouth, and he fed me the scroll. "Fill your stomach with this," he said. And when I ate it, it tasted as sweet as honey in my mouth. . . . Then he added, "Son of man, let all my words sink deep into your own heart first. Listen to them carefully for yourself."*

GALATIANS 5:22-23 | *The Holy Spirit produces this kind of fruit in our lives: love, joy, peace, patience, kindness, goodness, faithfulness, gentleness, and self-control.*

JAMES 4:2-3 | *You don't have what you want because you don't ask God for it. And even when you ask, you don't get it because your motives are all wrong—you want only what will give you pleasure.*

Too many people try to meet their deepest needs in ways that just don't satisfy. The Bible often uses the analogy of food to explain what happens when you try to satisfy your desires in the wrong way. When you are hungry, it's because your body is craving good food, but eating only candy will never truly satisfy your cravings. You get shaky; you can't think straight; your body doesn't function right; and if you don't ever eat something healthy, you'll suffer long-term physical damage. The same principle applies to satisfying the hungry soul. If you fill it with only fun, pleasure, and sin, you'll always be craving something more. You'll throw your soul out of whack, and it won't function right. You need a steady diet of "soul" food—eating God's Word, thirsting for time with him so his Holy Spirit can fill you with the things that will make you a strong, mature man or woman of faith. Only God's way of life will truly satisfy your deepest cravings because God created you to be in relationship with him. When you have eaten well, you will have the strength and wisdom to take advantage of the opportunities God sends your way to truly make a difference, and you can be sure the satisfaction you feel will be sustained since it comes directly from God.

SEARCHING FOR GOD

How do I search for God? How do I form a relationship with him?

1 CHRONICLES 28:9 | *If you seek [the Lord], you will find him.*

PSALM 27:8 | *My heart has heard you say, "Come and talk with me." And my heart responds, "LORD, I am coming."*

PSALM 145:18 | *The LORD is close to all who call on him, yes, to all who call on him in truth.*

JAMES 4:8 | *Come close to God, and God will come close to you.*

When you have close friends, you do your best to stay in touch with them. You talk almost every day. One day you might call them, and the next day they'll call you. You might do things together you enjoy or just reminisce about past memories together. It's no different with God. A relationship with God requires effort, pursuit, frequent contact, and memories. When you're developing a relationship with him, try talking to him every day. Talk with him openly and honestly, as you would any close friend. Then take the time to listen. Allow a few moments each day for quality time with God, when you can express your concerns, talking about your future and remembering ways he's been with you and helped you in the past. Don't forget to ask him what he's doing, too, around the world and in your life. Read his Word, the Bible, daily to open yourself up to what God may be saying to you. Remember that God is with you all day, every day; talk to him about everything that comes up at home, at work, and everywhere else. Share your thoughts, needs, and concerns with him as they arise. As you get to know him by being with him every day, you'll begin to build memories with him and gain the relationship you desire. God promises that if you search for him, you'll find him, and you'll wonder how you ever got along without him.

SERVICE

Why is it so important to serve others?

MATTHEW 20:26, 28 | *[Jesus said,] "Whoever wants to be a leader among you must be your servant. . . . For even the Son of Man came not to be served but to serve others and to give his life as a ransom for many."*

MARK 10:43-44 | *[Jesus said,] "Whoever wants to be a leader among you must be your servant, and whoever wants to be first among you must be the slave of everyone else."*

GALATIANS 5:13 | *You have been called to live in freedom, my brothers and sisters. But don't use your freedom to satisfy your sinful nature. Instead, use your freedom to serve one another in love.*

EPHESIANS 3:20 | *All glory to God, who is able, through his mighty power at work within us, to accomplish infinitely more than we might ask or think.*

A popular notion of success in life is being able to afford the luxury of having servants. Jesus turns this thinking on its head by teaching that the highest goal in life is to *be* a servant. He places such a high value on serving because it is others-centered rather than self-centered; this is the essence of effective Christian living. When you are connected to Jesus, he turns your simple acts into something profound and purposeful. For example, he turns your simple act of singing into a profound chorus of praise that ministers to an entire congregation. He turns your simple act of placing your tithe in the offering plate into a profound act of mercy that will touch the heart of the needy person who receives it. He turns your simple act of teaching children in Sunday school into a profound moment in the heart of a child who suddenly realizes the need for salvation. He turns your simple act of visiting shut-ins into a divine moment of encouragement. When you step out to serve, God turns your simple acts of service into profound works for the Kingdom of God.

SIN

Isn't "sin" kind of an outdated word? What is "sin" really?

MATTHEW 15:18-19 | *The words you speak come from the heart—that's what defiles you. For from the heart come evil thoughts, murder, adultery, all sexual immorality, theft, lying, and slander.*

ROMANS 3:12 | *All have turned away; all have become useless. No one does good, not a single one.*

ROMANS 3:23 | *Everyone has sinned; we all fall short of God's glorious standard.*

GALATIANS 5:19-21 | *When you follow the desires of your sinful nature, the results are very clear: sexual immorality, impurity, lustful pleasures, idolatry, sorcery, hostility, quarreling, jealousy, outbursts of anger, selfish ambition, dissension, division, envy, drunkenness, wild parties, and other sins like these.*

JAMES 4:17 | *It is sin to know what you ought to do and then not do it.*

1 JOHN 1:9 | *If we confess our sins to him, he is faithful and just to forgive us our sins and to cleanse us from all wickedness.*

Sin will always be an offensive word. We can talk openly and impersonally about crimes such as robbery and murder; we can calculate statistics about adultery, unwed pregnancies, and divorces; we can trivialize greed, selfishness, and jealousy—or call them cultural values; but to call anything "sin" makes us uncomfortable. The word *sin* implies the violation of an objective and absolute standard of behavior established by God. We almost instinctively feel this to be an infringement on our rights. Yet such an attitude displays a terrible misunderstanding of sin and an underestimation of God. When a doctor correctly diagnoses a disease in our bodies, we do not accuse him or her of impinging on our freedom; rather, we are grateful because the doctor will know how to treat the disease before it destroys our lives.

The Bible teaches that sin is a disease of the soul that has spread to all humankind. It will destroy your life and lead to spiritual death if you do not treat it. God's standard of behavior is preventive medicine, prescribed not to limit your freedom but to curtail the disease of sin. And ironically, the antidote for sin is not only free but also comes with the free gift of eternal life. The fact that such a bargain from God is so hard to accept shows just how enticing and enslaving sin can be.

1 PETER 2:24 | *[Christ] personally carried our sins in his body on the cross so that we can be dead to sin and live for what is right. By his wounds you are healed.*

If there were no consequences for driving through red lights, breaking into people's homes, or killing people, anarchy would reign. The things people value most—peace, order, security—would be gone. Sin is breaking the laws that the Creator of the universe set up to bring peace, order, and security to the world. Breaking God's laws brings God's punishment, just as breaking government laws brings civil punishment. The good news is this: When Jesus died on the cross, he took the punishment for sin that you deserve. Sin no longer controls you; God gives you the power to overcome sin and live the way he meant life to be lived. To be "dead to sin" doesn't mean that you won't sin anymore in this life; it means that you have come to the point where you truly don't want to sin. You really want to please God and do what is right. When you get to that point, you have understood how to use God's power in you to live effectively for him. And one day sin will be gone forever.

Am I really a Christian if I still sin?

JOHN 16:33 | *[Jesus said,] "I have told you all this so that you may have peace in me. Here on earth you will have many trials and sorrows. But take heart, because I have overcome the world."*

ROMANS 7:20 | *If I do what I don't want to do, I am not really the one doing wrong; it is sin living in me that does it.*

You will always struggle with sin, for no one is perfect. But if you have placed your faith in Jesus, he guarantees victory over sin. All Christians sin. But because you are a Christian, you have the help of Jesus Christ to keep sin from controlling you—and in the next life, to have overcome it forever.

ROMANS 8:5 | *Those who are dominated by the sinful nature think about sinful things, but those who are controlled by the Holy Spirit think about things that please the Spirit.*

Sin loses its influence over you as you increasingly yield your life to the control of the Holy Spirit. The Spirit of God living in you reduces your appetite for sin and increases your hunger for God.

I've done some horrible things. Could God possibly forgive me?

MATTHEW 18:21-22 | *Peter . . . asked, "Lord, how often should I forgive someone who sins against me? Seven times?" "No, not seven times," Jesus replied, "but seventy times seven!"*

EPHESIANS 1:7 | *[God] is so rich in kindness and grace that he purchased our freedom with the blood of his Son and forgave our sins.*

No matter how terrible your past or how many sins you have committed, if you approach God with an attitude of humble sincerity and confess your sins, he will forgive you. To think that some of your sins are too bad to be forgiven is to minimize the power of Jesus' death and resurrection on your behalf.

PSALM 103:3, 10-12 | *[The Lord] forgives all my sins. . . . He does not punish us for all our sins; he does not deal harshly with us, as we deserve. For his unfailing love toward those who fear him is as great as the height of the heavens above the earth. He has removed our sins as far from us as the east is from the west.*

JOEL 2:32 | *Everyone who calls on the name of the LORD will be saved.*

MARK 3:28 | *[Jesus said,] "I tell you the truth, all sin . . . can be forgiven."*

ROMANS 8:38 | *Nothing can ever separate us from God's love. Neither death nor life, neither angels nor demons, neither our fears for today nor our worries about tomorrow—not even the powers of hell can separate us from God's love.*

Forgiveness is not based on the magnitude of the sin but on the magnitude of the forgiver's love. No sin is too great for God's complete and unconditional love.

Why would God want to forgive me for a terrible sin?

NUMBERS 14:19 | *In keeping with your magnificent, unfailing love, please pardon the sins of this people.*

God's love is his motivation for his forgiveness. He wants a relationship with you more than anything, and he is happy to forgive you for any sin, no matter how terrible, if you simply long for a closer relationship with him and seek his forgiveness.

SOCIAL JUSTICE

Does God really care about the poor and the oppressed?

PSALM 35:10 | *LORD, who can compare with you? Who else rescues the helpless from the strong? Who else protects the helpless and poor from those who rob them?*

PSALM 72:12 | *He will rescue the poor when they cry to him; he will help the oppressed, who have no one to defend them.*

PSALM 113:6-8 | *He stoops to look down on heaven and on earth. He lifts the poor from the dust and the needy from the garbage dump. He sets them among princes.*

ISAIAH 25:4 | *You are a tower of refuge to the poor, O LORD, a tower of refuge to the needy in distress. You are a refuge from the storm and a shelter from the heat. For the oppressive acts of ruthless people are like a storm beating against a wall.*

AMOS 5:24 | *[The Lord says,] "I want to see a mighty flood of justice, an endless river of righteous living."*

ROMANS 8:35, 37 | *Does it mean he no longer loves us if we have trouble or calamity, or are persecuted, or hungry, or destitute, or in danger, or threatened with death? . . . No, despite all these things, overwhelming victory is ours through Christ, who loved us.*

God cares deeply for the poor and the oppressed. He commands all believers to care for them too. In fact, one test of godliness is your care for them. Conversely, if you are poor or are oppressed—such as suffering from a crippling disease, grieving over the loss of a loved one, feeling lonely or abandoned, or living in constant danger—your greatest hope as a believer is that this condition is temporary. God promises that the time will come when you will be free from all trouble for eternity (see Revelation 21:4).

SPIRITUAL DISCIPLINES

What are "spiritual disciplines," and are they really important?

JEREMIAH 29:13 | *[The Lord says,] "If you look for me whole-heartedly, you will find me."*

1 TIMOTHY 4:8 | *Physical training is good, but training for godliness is much better, promising benefits in this life and in the life to come.*

Spiritual disciplines include prayer, fasting, solitude, stewardship, simplicity, and meditating on Scripture, to name a few. As you make these practices a regular part of your life, your relationship with God will be more vital and life changing, even when your circumstances are unsettled. You get close—and stay close—to God through regular practice of the spiritual disciplines. They are not ends in themselves; rather, they are the means by which you strengthen your connection with God and become more like him.

MATTHEW 4:2 I *For forty days and forty nights [Jesus] fasted and became very hungry.*

MARK 1:35 I *Before daybreak . . . Jesus got up and went out to an isolated place to pray.*

LUKE 5:16 I *Jesus often withdrew to the wilderness for prayer.*

The spiritual disciplines were central to Jesus' earthly life. If the Son of God relied on them to stay connected to God, they must be important.

How can I maintain spiritual vitality?

PROVERBS 4:23 I *Guard your heart above all else, for it determines the course of your life.*

Every aspect of your life is affected by the spiritual condition of your heart. Because of the impact you can make on others, you must care for your inner life. Otherwise, your weaknesses, wounds, and weariness will likely affect those around you in negative ways. And on the other hand, your spiritual vitality will inspire and sustain those around you. The spiritual disciplines are the ways you can care for your heart and soul. You do not practice them to impress God but rather to allow God to impress himself on you. They are not achievements you perform for God but ways you make yourself available to him.

1 CORINTHIANS 9:24-27 | *Don't you realize that in a race everyone runs, but only one person gets the prize? So run to win! All athletes are disciplined in their training. They do it to win a prize that will fade away, but we do it for an eternal prize. So I run with purpose in every step. I am not just shadowboxing. I discipline my body like an athlete, training it to do what it should. Otherwise, I fear that after preaching to others I myself might be disqualified.*

An athlete trains over and over again so that fundamental actions become almost automatic. In the same way, spiritual disciplines need to be developed until they become reflexes.

1 TIMOTHY 4:7-10 | *Do not waste time arguing over godless ideas and old wives' tales. Instead, train yourself to be godly. "Physical training is good, but training for godliness is much better, promising benefits in this life and in the life to come." This is a trustworthy saying, and everyone should accept it. This is why we work hard and continue to struggle, for our hope is in the living God, who is the Savior of all people and particularly of all believers.*

Spiritual disciplines not only prepare you for this life but also develop your heart and soul for eternity. That's why you must take time for spiritual development and conditioning.

ISAIAH 1:12-17 | *When you come to worship me, who asked you to parade through my courts with all your ceremony? Stop*

bringing me your meaningless gifts; the incense of your offer-
ings disgusts me! As for your celebrations of the new moon and
the Sabbath and your special days for fasting— they are all
sinful and false. I want no more of your pious meetings. I hate
your new moon celebrations and your annual festivals. They
are a burden to me. I cannot stand them! When you lift up
your hands in prayer, I will not look. Though you offer many
prayers, I will not listen, for your hands are covered with the
blood of innocent victims. Wash yourselves and be clean! Get
your sins out of my sight. Give up your evil ways. Learn to
do good. Seek justice. Help the oppressed. Defend the cause of
orphans. Fight for the rights of widows.

It's important to remember that the spiritual disciplines
cannot take the place of a heart committed to God. They
become hypocrisy when not motivated by godliness.

SPIRITUAL DRYNESS

How can I prevent spiritual dryness?

PSALM 63:1 | *O God, you are my God; I earnestly search for*
you. My soul thirsts for you; my whole body longs for you in
this parched and weary land where there is no water.

JOHN 7:37 | *Jesus stood and shouted to the crowds, "Anyone*
who is thirsty may come to me!"

A tree close to a riverbank grows full and tall. In the same way,
if you stay close to God you will grow to spiritual maturity. You
will not hunger or thirst for meaning in life because God will
nourish you with his Word and his presence. You stay close to

God by being with him consistently and persistently through reading the Bible, praying, spending time with other believers, and serving him in a church and other ministries.

1 JOHN 5:21 | *Keep away from anything that might take God's place in your hearts.*

Keep sin from taking a foothold in your life. Sin always leads you away from God. To avoid drifting from God, guard your affection for and devotion to him.

PSALM 32:3-4 | *When I refused to confess my sin, my body wasted away, and I groaned all day long. Day and night your hand of discipline was heavy on me. My strength evaporated like water in the summer heat.*

Confess any sin right away, and ask God to forgive you and turn your heart back toward him.

PHILIPPIANS 2:4 | *Don't look out only for your own interests, but take an interest in others, too.*

Practice genuine, active love for those around you. Love waters a dry soul.

SPIRITUAL GIFTS

What are spiritual gifts? How do I use them for God?

ISAIAH 6:8 | *I heard the Lord asking, "Whom should I send as a messenger to this people? Who will go for us?" I said, "Here I am. Send me."*

1 CORINTHIANS 12:7-9, 22 | *A spiritual gift is given to each of us so we can help each other. To one person the Spirit gives*

the ability to give wise advice; to another the same Spirit gives a message of special knowledge. The same Spirit gives great faith to another, and to someone else the one Spirit gives the gift of healing. . . . In fact, some parts of the body that seem weakest and least important are actually the most necessary.

2 TIMOTHY 1:6-7 | *Fan into flames the spiritual gift God gave you. . . . For God has not given us a spirit of fear and timidity, but of power, love, and self-discipline.*

1 PETER 4:10 | *God has given each of you a gift from his great variety of spiritual gifts. Use them well to serve one another.*

Being available to God includes the continual development of the gifts he has given you so that you will be prepared for him to use you. It involves your willingness to use those gifts to serve him in the calling he currently has for you. Do you know the unique gifts God has given you? If not, find a spiritual gifts assessment—this test should help you discover what your gifts are. Also ask your friends what they think your gifts are. It is important to know that God gives each individual a spiritual gift (sometimes more than one!) and a special ministry in the church. These specific spiritual gifts help you fulfill the purpose for which God made you, and they help and encourage others and bring glory to his name. You never use these spiritual gifts up; rather, the more you use them, the more they grow and allow you to make a unique contribution in your sphere of influence. Using your spiritual gifts allows you to find the place where you can be most effective for God and where you do your best work for God in helping others.

SPIRITUAL WARFARE

Is spiritual warfare a reality?

MATTHEW 13:39 | *The enemy who planted the weeds among the wheat is the devil.*

EPHESIANS 6:12 | *We are not fighting against flesh-and-blood enemies, but against evil rulers and authorities of the unseen world, against mighty powers in this dark world, and against evil spirits in the heavenly places.*

Satan is alive and active, and his legions of demons are always on the attack. A battle rages in the spiritual realm —a battle you can't see, but one you will experience if you seek to serve God. You need God's power, not your own, to stand strong and not allow temptation to overcome you. Most of all, since you do not always know or understand the evil that is threatening you, you need God's power to give you strength to face an unknown enemy. Have peace that God has already won the battle over death and has the power to save you from evil.

GENESIS 3:1 | *The serpent was the shrewdest of all the wild animals the LORD God had made. One day he asked the woman, "Did God really say you must not eat the fruit from any of the trees in the garden?"*

2 KINGS 6:15-17 | *When the servant of the man of God got up early the next morning and went outside, there were troops, horses, and chariots everywhere. "Oh, sir, what will we do now?" the young man cried to Elisha. "Don't be afraid!" Elisha told him. "For there are more on our side than on theirs!" Then*

Elisha prayed, "O LORD, open his eyes and let him see!" The LORD opened the young man's eyes, and when he looked up, he saw that the hillside around Elisha was filled with horses and chariots of fire.

MATTHEW 4:1 | *Jesus was led by the Spirit into the wilderness to be tempted there by the devil.*

1 PETER 5:8-9 | *Stay alert! Watch out for your great enemy, the devil. He prowls around like a roaring lion, looking for someone to devour. Stand firm against him, and be strong in your faith.*

The Bible clearly teaches that, from the beginning of time and exemplified in Jesus' own ministry, human beings are involved in spiritual warfare. Far from excluding you from spiritual battles, faith puts you right in the middle of them. Those who underestimate this put themselves in jeopardy.

PHILIPPIANS 2:10 | *At the name of Jesus every knee should bow, in heaven and on earth and under the earth.*

JAMES 4:7 | *Resist the devil, and he will flee from you.*

When you resist the devil in the name and power of Jesus, he will flee from you. At the name of Jesus, Satan has no power.

In spiritual warfare, how do I fight?

MATTHEW 4:4, 7, 10 | *Jesus told [Satan], "No! The Scriptures say . . .". . . Jesus [said], "The Scriptures also say . . ." "Get out of here, Satan," Jesus told him. "For the Scriptures say . . ."*

EPHESIANS 6:10-12 | *Be strong in the Lord and in his mighty power. Put on all of God's armor so that you will be able to stand firm against all strategies of the devil. For we are not fighting against flesh-and-blood enemies, but against evil rulers and authorities of the unseen world, against mighty powers in this dark world, and against evil spirits in the heavenly places.*

EPHESIANS 6:17 I *Take the sword of the Spirit, which is the word of God.*

2 THESSALONIANS 3:3 I *The Lord is faithful; he will strengthen you and guard you from the evil one.*

Your best offensive weapon is the Word of God. It's odd to think of the Bible as a weapon, but in it, God reveals his plan of attack against evil. It's your battle plan as well; if you don't read the Bible, you won't know how to fight the battle that literally determines your destiny, here on earth and for eternity. The Bible exposes the enemy, Satan, for who he is, shines the light of truth on his lies, teaches you how to prepare for his attacks, and makes you wise against his tricks and strategies. Only by knowing who you are fighting, where the battle is, and how to defend yourself will you be able to win. It is vital to read God's Word as regularly as possible. This weapon will send Satan running for cover.

STEWARDSHIP

What does it mean to be a good steward?

GENESIS 1:26 I *God said, "Let us make human beings in our image, to be like us. They will reign over the fish in the sea, the birds in the sky, the livestock, all the wild animals on the earth, and the small animals that scurry along the ground."*

LEVITICUS 25:23 | *[The Lord said,] "The land belongs to me. You are only foreigners and tenant farmers working for me."*

PSALM 89:8, 11 | *O LORD God of Heaven's Armies! . . . The heavens are yours, and the earth is yours; everything in the world is yours—you created it all.*

MATTHEW 24:45-47 | *A faithful, sensible servant is one to whom the master can give the responsibility of managing his other household servants and feeding them. If the master returns and finds that the servant has done a good job, there will be a reward. I tell you the truth, the master will put that servant in charge of all he owns.*

ROMANS 14:12 | *Each of us will give a personal account to God.*

Most of us think about money every day. Will we have enough to pay the bills? Where can we save? Can we pay less for this item somewhere else? How much will our monthly expenses be? When we carefully think about our money and try to spend and save it wisely, we are showing good stewardship of our financial resources. But often we forget that God calls us to be good stewards of *all* the gifts he has provided for us to use and enjoy. For example, God has given us the earth and all its precious resources to manage responsibly. Since he has invested so much in us, as evidenced by his amazing plan of salvation and eternal life, we should invest our time and talents in his work and in other people—all he has given us—until he returns. The goal of stewardship is to make the best possible use of what we have in order to make the greatest possible impact on others, moving God's work forward as efficiently and effectively as possible.

How does God want me to use the resources available to me?

MATTHEW 25:21 | *The master was full of praise. "Well done, my good and faithful servant. You have been faithful in handling this small amount, so now I will give you many more responsibilities."*

God wants you to use what you are given faithfully.

PHILEMON 1:6 | *Put into action the generosity that comes from your faith as you understand and experience all the good things we have in Christ.*

Share what you have with a generous heart as often as you can.

ECCLESIASTES 11:6 | *Plant your seed in the morning and keep busy all afternoon, for you don't know if profit will come from one activity or another—or maybe both.*

Prepare for the future by wisely managing what is entrusted to you.

DEUTERONOMY 16:17 | *All must give as they are able, according to the blessings given to them by the LORD your God.*

PROVERBS 3:9 | *Honor the LORD with your wealth and with the best part of everything you produce.*

Give to God's servants and God's work, even to the point of sacrifice.

PROVERBS 3:27-28 | *Do not withhold good from those who deserve it when it's in your power to help them. If you can help your neighbor now, don't say, "Come back tomorrow, and then I'll help you."*

LUKE 3:11 | *If you have two shirts, give one to the poor. If you have food, share it with those who are hungry.*

ROMANS 12:13 | *When God's people are in need, be ready to help them. Always be eager to practice hospitality.*

Use your resources to help those who are in need.

1 CORINTHIANS 6:19-20 | *Don't you realize that your body is the temple of the Holy Spirit, who lives in you and was given to you by God? You do not belong to yourself, for God bought you with a high price. So you must honor God with your body.*

Take care of your body so you will be strong and healthy to serve God and others.

LUKE 12:48 | *When someone has been given much, much will be required in return; and when someone has been entrusted with much, even more will be required.*

1 CORINTHIANS 9:16 | *Preaching the Good News is not something I can boast about. I am compelled by God to do it. How terrible for me if I didn't preach the Good News!*

You are will be held accountable to God for the use of your gifts and opportunities. God entrusts resources to you and expects you to maximize the effectiveness of your abilities in wise and godly stewardship. Though you may think that the most talented people seem the most blessed, remember that they are also required to be the most responsible.

SUFFERING

I've heard it said that good can come from suffering. How does that happen?

ROMANS 5:3-4 | *We can rejoice . . . when we run into problems and trials, for we know that they help us develop endurance. And endurance develops strength of character.*

2 CORINTHIANS 1:3-4 | *All praise to God, the Father of our Lord Jesus Christ. God is our merciful Father and the source of all comfort. He comforts us in all our troubles.*

2 CORINTHIANS 4:18 | *We don't look at the troubles we can see now; rather, we fix our gaze on things that cannot be seen. For the things we see now will soon be gone, but the things we cannot see will last forever.*

1 PETER 5:10 | *In his kindness God called you to share in his eternal glory by means of Christ Jesus. So after you have suffered a little while, he will restore, support, and strengthen you, and he will place you on a firm foundation.*

It makes sense that you, living in a pleasure-seeking society, would try to avoid suffering at any cost. But it is through suffering, as with other challenges, that you grow. You don't like pain and adversity because they challenge you physically, mentally, emotionally, and spiritually. But those who have gone through such taxing times are stronger and wiser because of them. An athlete or a musician will never achieve greatness without painful hours of practice. Likewise, you will never become strong and wise without being pushed, shoved, and hurt by life's troubles. While God never enjoys seeing you suffer, he sometimes allows painful and adverse times in your life in order to strengthen your character. God uses suffering to expand your perspective and turn your thoughts heavenward, to strengthen your faith as you wait expectantly for his promises to come true. Often it is not until you reach the other side of suffering that you can appreciate the perspective and growth achieved.

What are God's promises in the midst of suffering?

ISAIAH 43:1-2 | *Do not be afraid, for I have ransomed you. I have called you by name; you are mine. When you go through deep waters, I will be with you. When you go through rivers of difficulty, you will not drown. When you walk through the fire of oppression, you will not be burned up; the flames will not consume you.*

ROMANS 8:38-39 | *Nothing can ever separate us from God's love. Neither death nor life, neither angels nor demons, neither our fears for today nor our worries about tomorrow—not even the powers of hell can separate us from God's love. No power in the sky above or in the earth below—indeed, nothing in all creation will ever be able to separate us from the love of God that is revealed in Christ Jesus our Lord.*

When you are suffering, the greatest comfort in life is knowing that God will never leave you. Nothing can drive his presence away from you. You may go through deep waters of trouble and intense fires of trial and testing, but you will not go through them alone. No matter what you are going through, he's there to comfort, sustain, encourage, and direct you.

How do I explain suffering to someone who is hurting?

LUKE 10:30, 34 | *A Jewish man was traveling from Jerusalem down to Jericho, and he was attacked by bandits. They stripped him of his clothes, beat him up, and left him half dead beside the road. . . . Going over to him, the Samaritan soothed his wounds with olive oil and wine and bandaged them. Then he put the man on his own donkey and took him to an inn, where he took care of him.*

ROMANS 12:15 | *Be happy with those who are happy, and weep with those who weep.*

1 CORINTHIANS 12:26 | *If one part suffers, all the parts suffer with it, and if one part is honored, all the parts are glad.*

2 CORINTHIANS 1:3-4 | *All praise to God, the Father of our Lord Jesus Christ. God is our merciful Father and the source of all comfort. He comforts us in all our troubles so that we can comfort others. When they are troubled, we will be able to give them the same comfort God has given us.*

GALATIANS 6:2 | *Share each other's burdens, and in this way obey the law of Christ.*

Suffering is a universal experience. Some suffering comes by chance, such as car accidents that maim or illnesses that ravage loved ones or even take their lives. Some suffering happens by neglect, such as our failure to prepare for times of pressure. Sometimes it is by design, when we willingly take on enormous responsibilities in order to achieve a goal. Other times it is by sin, when we stubbornly go against God's commands and then suffer the consequences.

Whatever the source, at times we all feel the dark shadow of suffering, and we don't know how to explain it. But maybe we don't have to. The reality is that we don't usually know why suffering has struck us or someone else, and one of the worst mistakes we can make is to try to explain it out of ignorance. We do know two things about suffering: (1) It hurts deeply, causing much grief and distress; and (2) comfort comes from those who love us and sit with us, not those who lecture us and try to fix it.

When you join in someone else's suffering, you are

choosing to be wounded with him or her, and that brings comfort. If you know someone who is hurting, suffer along with that person to bring comfort and hope.

SURRENDER

What does it mean to surrender my life to God?

MARK 8:34-35 | *[Jesus] said, "If any of you wants to be my follower, you must turn from your selfish ways, take up your cross, and follow me. If you try to hang on to your life, you will lose it. But if you give up your life for my sake and for the sake of the Good News, you will save it."*

LUKE 14:33 | *[Jesus said,] "You cannot become my disciple without giving up everything you own."*

When you surrender to God, you give up what you want in order to receive what God has planned for you. Jesus is not saying you *have* to give up everything to follow him but that you must be *willing* to give up everything to follow him. Only when you are willing to give up everything for God will you be able to receive everything he wants to offer you. It all comes down to control. How often have you foolishly fought against God and his will for you because you want to have ultimate control over your life? This is when surrender is necessary and positive. Surrender to God comes when you at last realize you are powerless to run your life and to defeat sin by yourself, and you give control of your life to God. Then you can be victorious in your battle to defeat sin, and you will experience the greatest freedom possible as you pursue the goal of victory in this life and for eternity.

TEMPTATION

How do I learn to recognize temptation? Why is it so enticing to me?

GENESIS 3:1, 6 | *The serpent was the shrewdest of all the wild animals the LORD God had made. One day he asked the woman, "Did God really say . . . ?" . . . The woman was convinced. She saw that the . . . fruit looked delicious, and she wanted the wisdom it would give her. So she took some of the fruit and ate it.*

2 CORINTHIANS 11:14-15 | *Satan disguises himself as an angel of light. So it is no wonder that his servants also disguise themselves as servants of righteousness. In the end they will get the punishment their wicked deeds deserve.*

Satan's favorite strategies are to make sin look desirable and good and to convince you that what is really true is false. He is the master of disguise. He will trick you into believing that if it feels right, it must be right; that pleasure is always good; and that truth is whatever works for you. If Satan can make evil look good and good look evil, then your giving in to temptation appears right instead of wrong. You must constantly be aware of the confusion he desires to create in you.

1 KINGS 11:1-3 | *Solomon loved many foreign women. . . . The LORD had clearly instructed the people of Israel, "You must not marry them, because they will turn your hearts to their gods." Yet Solomon insisted on loving them anyway. He had 700 wives of royal birth and 300 concubines. And in fact, they did turn his heart away from the LORD.*

Often temptation begins in seemingly harmless pleasure, soon gets out of control, and progresses to full-blown idolatry. But the reality is that the kind of pleasure that leads to sin is never harmless. Before you give in to something that seems innocent, take a look into God's Word for a reality check. If Solomon had done this, he would have been reminded that his "pleasure" was really sin—the Bible is clear about staying committed to one woman in marriage and about the dangers of alliances with those who oppose God's ways. Maybe if Solomon had spent more time in God's Word, he would have decided to obey God and thus would have prevented his life from becoming a wreck.

MATTHEW 4:1, 3-11 | *Jesus was led by the Spirit into the wilderness. . . . During that time the devil came and said to him, "If you are the Son of God, tell these stones to become loaves of bread." But Jesus told him, "No! The Scriptures say, 'People do not live by bread alone, but by every word that comes from the mouth of God.'" Then the devil took him to the holy city, Jerusalem, to the highest point of the Temple, and said, "If you are the Son of God, jump off! For the Scriptures say, 'He will order his angels to protect you. And they will hold you up with their hands so you won't even hurt your foot on a stone.'" Jesus responded, "The Scriptures also say, 'You must not test the LORD your God.'" Next the devil took him to the peak of a very high mountain and showed him all the kingdoms of the world and their glory. "I will give it all to you," he said, "if you will kneel down and worship me." "Get out of here, Satan," Jesus told him. "For the Scriptures say, 'You must worship the LORD your God and serve only him.'" Then the devil went away, and angels came and took care of Jesus.*

Temptation often offers attractive short-term benefits but with destructive, even deadly, long-term consequences. Temptation is often convincingly seasoned with partial truths twisted into lies. Get to know God's truth so that anything that is not his truth will be easier to recognize.

Is temptation sin?

MATTHEW 4:1 | *Then Jesus was . . . tempted there by the devil.*

HEBREWS 4:15 | *[Jesus] understands our weaknesses, for he faced all of the same testings we do, yet he did not sin.*

Jesus was severely tempted, yet he never gave in to it. Since Jesus was tempted and remained sinless, being tempted is not the same as sinning. You don't have to feel guilty about the temptations you wrestle with. Rather, you can devote yourself to resisting them.

How can I have the power to resist temptation?

1 TIMOTHY 4:7-8 | *Train yourself to be godly. "Physical training is good, but training for godliness is much better, promising benefits in this life and in the life to come."*

To overcome temptation, you need to prepare for it before it presses in on you. Train yourself in the quieter times so that you will have the spiritual wisdom, strength, and commitment to honor God in the face of intense desires and temptation.

1 CORINTHIANS 10:13 | *The temptations in your life are no different from what others experience. . . . When you are tempted, [God] will show you a way out so that you can endure.*

1 JOHN 4:4 | *The Spirit who lives in you is greater than the spirit who lives in the world.*

1 JOHN 5:4-5 | *Every child of God defeats this evil world, and we achieve this victory through our faith. And who can win this battle against the world? Only those who believe that Jesus is the Son of God.*

Satan has the power to overwhelm you if you are alone. But against Jesus he becomes a coward. When Jesus lives in you in the form of the Holy Spirit, his power becomes available to you, and then *Satan* is overwhelmed. Now you have the advantage in overcoming any temptation. The devil can tempt you, but he cannot coerce you. He can dangle the bait in front of you, but he cannot force you to take it. He'll try every trick in the book to make you think you're missing out, that you cannot and should not resist.

But you can break free from temptation when you change your focus from what's in front of you to who is inside of you. Then you can discern the difference between the lies of the tempter and the truth of God's Word, between what seems so right and what's really right. So instead of thinking about missing out on something, think about what you'll be gaining by moving in God's direction. You have far more power available to you than you think. When you arm yourself with God's Word and rely on the presence of his Spirit within you, temptations become divine moments in which you can experience the power of God helping you resist.

JAMES 4:7 | *Humble yourselves before God. Resist the devil, and he will flee from you.*

Satan's great passion is to get you to do anything that does not involve God. He will try to get you to ignore God, forget about God, be apathetic about God, deny God, doubt God, and sin against God. If you give Satan an inch, he will attack you even harder. But if you ignore Satan, neglect him, passionately fight against him, deny him, and resist him, eventually he may want to bother someone else who is an easier target. He will avoid you more if he gets the clear message that he cannot win you over.

ECCLESIASTES 4:12 | *A person standing alone can be attacked and defeated, but two can stand back-to-back and conquer. Three are even better, for a triple-braided cord is not easily broken.*

Enlisting a Christian friend as an accountability partner will give you far more spiritual strength than you have on your own.

Does temptation ever come from God?

JAMES 1:13 | *When you are being tempted, do not say, "God is tempting me." God is never tempted to do wrong, and he never tempts anyone else.*

Temptation originates not in the mind of God but in the mind of Satan, who plants it in your heart. Victory over temptation originates in the mind of God and flows to your heart.

ROMANS 5:3-4 | *We can rejoice, too, when we run into problems and trials, for we know that they help us develop endurance. And endurance develops strength of character, and character strengthens our confident hope of salvation.*

JAMES 1:2 | *When troubles come your way, consider it an opportunity for great joy.*

Although God does not send temptation, he brings good from it by helping you grow stronger through it.

How do I recover when I have given in to temptation?

1 JOHN 1:9 | *If we confess our sins to him, he is faithful and just to forgive us our sins and to cleanse us.*

God's grace is greater than your failure. His forgiveness overcomes your sin. Temptation only wins when it keeps you from turning back to God. Confess your sin to God, ask for his forgiveness, accept it, and recommit yourself to obedience. Then make every effort to stay away from what got you into trouble. No matter how often you fail, God welcomes you back through the love of Jesus Christ.

TESTING

How is testing different from temptation?

1 PETER 1:7 | *These trials will show that your faith is genuine. It is being tested as fire tests and purifies gold—though your faith is far more precious than mere gold. So when your faith remains strong through many trials, it will bring you much praise and glory and honor on the day when Jesus Christ is revealed to the whole world.*

Satan tempts to destroy your faith, but God tests to strengthen and purify it.

JAMES 1:3 | *When your faith is tested, your endurance has a chance to grow.*

Temptations try to make you quit. Testing helps you endure and not quit.

What are some of the ways that God tests me?

HEBREWS 11:8 | *It was by faith that Abraham obeyed when God called him to leave home and go to another land that God would give him as his inheritance. He went without knowing where he was going.*

God may test you through incomplete information to see how strong your faith in him really is. Just as you don't need to know everything about electricity to turn on a light, so you need not know everything about God's ways to trust his promises that he will do what is best for you.

2 CHRONICLES 32:31 | *When ambassadors arrived from Babylon to ask about the remarkable events that had taken place in the land, God withdrew from Hezekiah in order to test him and to see what was really in his heart.*

God may test you through silence. Sometimes what God doesn't say may be more effective in getting your attention.

GENESIS 22:1-3, 9-12 | *God tested Abraham's faith. "Abraham!" God called. "Yes," he replied. "Here I am." "Take your son . . . and sacrifice him as a burnt offering on one of the mountains, which I will show you." The next morning Abraham got up . . . and set out for the place God had told him about. . . . When they arrived at the place, . . . Abraham built an altar and arranged the wood on it. Then he tied his son, Isaac, and laid him on the altar. . . . Abraham picked up the knife to kill his son as a sacrifice. At that moment the angel of the LORD called to him from heaven, "Abraham! Abraham!" "Yes," Abraham replied. "Here I am!" "Don't lay a hand on the boy!" the angel said. "Do not hurt him in any way, for now I know that you truly fear God. You have not withheld from me even your son, your only son."*

God may test you through sacrifice. What you give up for God reveals more than what you keep for yourself.

ACTS 5:41-42 | *The apostles left the high council rejoicing that God had counted them worthy to suffer disgrace for the name of Jesus. And every day, in the Temple and from house to house, they continued to teach and preach this message: "Jesus is the Messiah."*

God may test you through problems and trials, even persecution. While no one wants troubles in life, most of us desire the healthy benefits and rewards they bring.

2 CORINTHIANS 12:7-9 | *To keep me from becoming proud, I was given a thorn in my flesh. . . . Three different times I begged the Lord to take it away. Each time he said, "My grace is all you need. My power works best in weakness." So now I am glad to boast about my weaknesses, so that the power of Christ can work through me.*

God may test you through your weaknesses. Only when you acknowledge your weaknesses can you invite God's strength to work through you.

PSALM 26:1-3 | *Declare me innocent, O LORD, for I have acted with integrity; I have trusted in the LORD without wavering. Put me on trial, LORD, and cross-examine me. Test my motives*

and my heart. For I am always aware of your unfailing love,
and I have lived according to your truth.

God may test you through life choices. The road you choose
will always determine the destination you reach. The
choices you make will always determine the consequences.

THANKFULNESS

Why is thankfulness such an important attitude?

PSALM 50:23 | *[God says,] "Giving thanks is a sacrifice that*
truly honors me. If you keep to my path, I will reveal to you
the salvation of God."

PSALM 92:1 | *It is good to give thanks to the LORD, to sing*
praises to the Most High.

HABAKKUK 3:17-19 | *Even though the fig trees have no blossoms,*
and there are no grapes on the vines; even though the olive
crop fails, and the fields lie empty and barren; even though the
flocks die in the fields, and the cattle barns are empty, yet I will
rejoice in the LORD! I will be joyful in the God of my salvation!
The Sovereign LORD is my strength! He makes me as surefooted
as a deer, able to tread upon the heights.

1 THESSALONIANS 5:18 | *Be thankful in all circumstances, for this*
is God's will for you who belong to Christ Jesus.

Thankfulness changes the way you look at the circumstances
of your life: Gratitude and praise connect you to the source
of real joy; complaining connects you to unhappiness. When
you make thanksgiving a regular part of your life, you stay

focused on what God has done and continues to do for you. Expressing gratitude for God's help is a form of worship. When you give thanks to God, you honor and praise him for what he has done—in your life, in the lives of others, in the church, and in the world. Similarly, you honor others when you give thanks to them, respecting them for who they are and for what they have done. This attitude of gratitude prevents you from expecting others to serve you and allows you to enjoy whatever blessings come your way. An attitude of thankfulness not only brings blessings to your life but blesses others with appreciation and honor.

THOUGHT LIFE

How can I improve my thoughts so they are more pleasing to God?

JOSHUA 1:8 | *Study this Book of Instruction continually. Meditate on it day and night so you will be sure to obey everything written in it. Only then will you prosper and succeed in all you do.*

PSALM 119:11 | *I have hidden your word in my heart, that I might not sin against you.*

2 TIMOTHY 3:16 | *All Scripture is inspired by God and is useful to teach us what is true and to make us realize what is wrong in our lives. It corrects us when we are wrong and teaches us to do what is right.*

Spend regular time reading and studying the Bible. These are God's words to you. The more you fill yourself with the words of God, the less you are filled with wrong or harmful thoughts.

MATTHEW 5:28 | *Anyone who even looks at a woman with lust has already committed adultery with her in his heart.*

MARK 7:20-23 | *It is what comes from inside that defiles you. For from within, out of a person's heart, come evil thoughts, sexual immorality, theft, murder, adultery, greed, wickedness, deceit, lustful desires, envy, slander, pride, and foolishness. All these vile things come from within; they are what defile you.*

JAMES 5:16 | *Confess your sins to each other and pray for each other so that you may be healed. The earnest prayer of a righteous person has great power and produces wonderful results.*

Bad thoughts are going to pop into your mind; it's when you encourage them to stay that you get in trouble. When bad thoughts come to mind, don't dwell on them but immediately turn to God in prayer. After you do this a few times, turning to God with a quick prayer for help will start to become a habit.

PSALM 19:14 | *May the words of my mouth and the meditation of my heart be pleasing to you, O LORD, my rock and my redeemer.*

PSALM 26:2 | *Put me on trial, LORD, and cross-examine me. Test my motives and my heart.*

PSALM 139:23 | *Search me, O God, and know my heart; test me and know my anxious thoughts.*

ROMANS 12:2 | *Let God transform you into a new person by changing the way you think. Then you will learn to know God's will for you, which is good and pleasing and perfect.*

Develop a real desire to invite God into your thought life
so he can hold you accountable. Invite him into your mind,
and ask him to make you aware whenever bad thoughts
come to mind, even though there might be a part of you
that doesn't want him to do so. Eventually, you will start to
realize why the part of you that wants to do good spoke up.

TRUST

What does it really mean to trust God?

REVELATION 4:11 I *You are worthy, O Lord our God, to receive
glory and honor and power. For you created all things.*

Trusting God means recognizing that he is your Creator so
that he knows what is best for you.

EPHESIANS 3:17 I *Christ will make his home in your hearts as you
trust in him. Your roots will grow down into God's love and
keep you strong.*

Trusting God is an ongoing process based on a personal
relationship with him.

GENESIS 6:13-14, 17, 22 I *God said to Noah, . . . "Build a large
boat. . . . I am about to cover the earth with a flood." . . .
Noah did everything exactly as God had commanded him.*

Trusting God means obeying his commands even when
you don't fully understand why.

ROMANS 3:22 I *We are made right with God by placing our faith
in Jesus Christ. And this is true for everyone who believes, no
matter who we are.*

Trusting God means depending on Jesus Christ alone for salvation.

PROVERBS 3:5-7 | *Trust in the LORD with all your heart; do not depend on your own understanding. Seek his will in all you do, and he will show you which path to take. Don't be impressed with your own wisdom. Instead, fear the LORD and turn away from evil.*

1 PETER 5:7 | *Give all your worries and cares to God, for he cares about you.*

Trusting God is acknowledging that he knows what is best, that he has everything under control, and that you surrender to his plan.

PSALM 112:1 | *How joyful are those who fear the LORD and delight in obeying his commands.*

Trusting God gives you the confidence that obeying him is the best way to live.

1 PETER 1:8 | *Though you do not see [God] now, you trust him; and you rejoice.*

Trusting God means knowing he is there even though you can't see him.

TRUTH

What is really true? Is anything true anymore?

GENESIS 1:1 | *In the beginning God created the heavens and the earth.*

2 SAMUEL 7:28 | *You are God, O Sovereign LORD. Your words are truth.*

PSALM 19:7 | *The instructions of the LORD are perfect, reviving the soul. The decrees of the LORD are trustworthy, making wise the simple.*

PROVERBS 12:19 | *Truthful words stand the test of time, but lies are soon exposed.*

JOHN 14:6 | *Jesus [said], "I am the way, the truth, and the life. No one can come to the Father except through me."*

JOHN 18:37 | *[Jesus said,] "I was born and came into the world to testify to the truth. All who love the truth recognize that what I say is true."*

2 TIMOTHY 3:16 | *All Scripture is inspired by God and is useful to teach us what is true and to make us realize what is wrong in our lives. It corrects us when we are wrong and teaches us to do what is right.*

Few things impact our daily lives as much as the concept of truth. First, there's "telling the truth." We gravitate toward those who tell the truth because they can be trusted. Without trust, relationships fall apart. We have to be truthful if we want relationships to work, companies to work, and government to work. Second, there's absolute truth—fundamental principles of nature, science, and human behavior that were built into the universe from the beginning of time. For example, the truth (or law) of gravity is that when you drop an object it will fall. A truth of mathematics is that two plus two equals four. A truth of biology is that the right amounts of hydrogen and oxygen make water. A truth about life in general is that every person enters this world as a baby and someday exits this world through death. Only a fool would argue that these truths aren't real and valid. There is nothing any person can do to change these fundamental truths about how the world works. The Bible claims there is a third kind of truth: spiritual truth, which is made up of moral and supernatural principles about our relationship with God and others. These principles are absolute and constant despite our feelings and beliefs to the contrary. We as humans have always wanted to reserve the right to determine this kind of truth for ourselves or to believe it doesn't exist at all.

Ironically, it's this kind of truth that, while difficult to discover and to accept, will most affect the way you live here on earth as well as your eternal destiny. Just as you can't reject the truth about gravity and expect to function well in this world, so you can't reject the truth about God and how he has determined human life should work and then expect your future to turn out the way you want it to. It's wise to discover and study this kind of truth because it so completely impacts the life of every human being on the planet. You are free to ignore truth if you so choose, but you do so at your own risk, both now and for eternity.

UNITY

The Bible says a lot about the importance of unity among believers. What does true unity look like?

PSALM 34:14 | *Search for peace, and work to maintain it.*

1 CORINTHIANS 12:14, 18, 20 | *The body has many different parts, not just one part, . . . and God has put each part just where he wants it. . . . Yes, there are many parts, but only one body.*

GALATIANS 3:26-28 | *You are all children of God through faith in Christ Jesus. And all who have been united with Christ in baptism have put on Christ, like putting on new clothes. There is no longer Jew or Gentile, slave or free, male and female. For you are all one in Christ Jesus.*

EPHESIANS 4:3 | *Make every effort to keep yourselves united in the Spirit, binding yourselves together with peace.*

One of the keys to unity is celebrating one another's differences. Unity is not about everyone agreeing or having the same opinion. It's about learning how to take different opinions and direct them all toward a common purpose and goal. God creates everyone different, so we should expect differences of opinion. But God also tells us to be united, which means that our differences must serve the important goal of bringing about the most thoughtful, well-developed plans. Unity becomes difficult to achieve when we're convinced that our own opinion is the best and, therefore, that someone else's opinion is not well thought through. This mindset keeps us from listening to new ideas that might actually make the plan better. We are tuning out a potential divine moment in which God could help us see how different colors create a richer painting. We need to try celebrating and truly appreciating one another's differences and try fitting them together to accomplish godly objectives. Then we will experience the true harmony that God designed humans to share and enjoy.

VALUES

───────────────────────────────◄●

There's a lot of talk about values. Are they really so important?

2 CHRONICLES 19:9 | *You must always act in the fear of the LORD, with faithfulness and an undivided heart.*

PSALM 15:1-2 | *Who may worship in your sanctuary, LORD? Who may enter your presence on your holy hill? Those who lead blameless lives and do what is right, speaking the truth from sincere hearts.*

MATTHEW 6:24 | *No one can serve two masters. For you will hate one and love the other; you will be devoted to one and despise the other. You cannot serve both God and money.*

LUKE 12:34 | *Wherever your treasure is, there the desires of your heart will also be.*

1 CORINTHIANS 16:13 | *Be on guard. Stand firm in the faith. Be courageous. Be strong.*

How do you spend most of your free time? Who is your favorite entertainer? Who are your best friends? What do you think about the majority of the time? How do you spend your money? Your answers to these questions will show what you value most. Whatever you consider important, useful, and worth a lot is what you value. You may have heard someone described as having no values. But that's not true. Everyone has values, good and/or bad ones. The problem comes when you don't value what God says is best for you; instead, you let the world's values shape you. Your values are crystal clear to those around you, because what you do, how you spend your time and money, and what you talk about show exactly what you value. When you value God the most, this will be reflected in the words you speak and how you spend your time, energy, and money. When you love and worship the Lord, obey him wholeheartedly, trust him with your future, and serve others, you are displaying godly values, and your life will be purposeful in a powerful way.

WAITING

I try to faithfully follow Jesus. Why won't he give me more victories over the everyday problems I face?

DEUTERONOMY 7:22 | *The LORD your God will drive those nations out ahead of you little by little. You will not clear them away all at once, otherwise the wild animals would multiply too quickly for you.*

PSALM 37:7 | *Be still in the presence of the LORD, and wait patiently for him to act. Don't worry about evil people who prosper or fret about their wicked schemes.*

JOHN 16:12 | *[Jesus said,] "There is so much more I want to tell you, but you can't bear it now."*

God often asks you to wait while leading you along the path of progressive—not immediate—victory. Why? Sometimes this keeps you from the pride that often comes after success. Sometimes it saves you from defeat. And sometimes God makes you wait to prepare you for a special task he has for you. Waiting is never time wasted by God, so don't waste it by being anxious. Serve God as you wait for him to accomplish the next good thing in your life.

WARNINGS

How should I view God's warnings?

DEUTERONOMY 28:13 | *[Moses said to the people,] "If you listen to these commands of the LORD your God that I am giving you today, and if you carefully obey them, the LORD will make you the head and not the tail, and you will always be on top and never at the bottom."*

PSALM 19:9-11 | *The laws of the LORD are true; each one is fair. They are more desirable than gold, even the finest gold. They are sweeter than honey, even honey dripping from the comb. They are a warning to your servant, a great reward for those who obey them.*

JEREMIAH 6:10 | *To whom can I give warning? Who will listen when I speak? Their ears are closed, and they cannot hear. They scorn the word of the LORD. They don't want to listen at all.*

HEBREWS 3:7-8, 13, 15 | *The Holy Spirit says, "Today when you hear his voice, don't harden your hearts." . . . You must warn each other every day, while it is still "today," so that none of you will be deceived by sin and hardened against God. . . . Remember what it says: "Today when you hear his voice, don't harden your hearts as Israel did when they rebelled."*

The society you live in is full of warnings. A red light at an intersection warns you to stop. A poison label warns you to put that product out of the reach of children. An ambulance siren warns you to get out of the way. How you view these warnings is a matter of perspective. You can look at them as intrusions that prevent you from enjoying life, or you can look at them as blessings that protect you so you can enjoy life. God's warnings are designed to protect you from the consequences of foolish actions. For example, God's warning to avoid sexual immorality will prevent you from the possibility of a broken heart, a damaged relationship, an unplanned pregnancy, or a sexually transmitted disease. How tragic that all too often people view God's warnings as obstacles to freedom! When you do that, you rebel against the very things designed to protect you. God's warnings are his way of trying to save you from doing something you'll later regret.

WILL OF GOD

How do I discover God's will for my life?

PSALM 119:9 | *How can a young person stay pure? By obeying your word.*

PSALM 119:105 | *Your word is a lamp to guide my feet and a light for my path.*

PROVERBS 3:6 | *Seek his will in all you do, and he will show you which path to take.*

PHILIPPIANS 2:13 | *God is working in you, giving you the desire and the power to do what pleases him.*

1 THESSALONIANS 4:3 I *God's will is for you to be holy, so stay away from all sexual sin.*

"What is God's will for my life?" If you believe in God, you have probably asked this question many times. Sometimes "God's will" seems so vague, so hard to know. Why can't God just give a divine sign with an arrow saying "Go this way"? The truth is that God already has given you not just a sign but a whole set of directions that will keep you in his will. The Bible is God's written Word, and it contains hundreds of clear rules and guidelines for you to follow. Here are some of them: Worship God only, love your neighbors and your enemies, discover your spiritual gifts and use them, tell the truth, do not covet, do not steal, be sexually pure, remain faithful, teach your children spiritual truths, don't gossip, be generous, don't take God's name in vain, read his Word regularly, don't let money control you, let the Holy Spirit control your life—and the list goes on. These are all God's will for your life.

But in addition to these directions that God created for all people, he also created you for a specific purpose and he calls you to do certain specific tasks to make your little area of the world a better place. It is usually through steadily following his general directions that you discover the more specific directions he has for you. So, if you stay in the center of God's will every day, you can be sure that you will be in the center of his will twenty years from now. God's will for you today is to obey him, to serve others, to read his Word, and to do what is right. Do those things today, and you are doing God's will. Do those things tomorrow and every day after that, and you will never be out of his will.

Then, when he calls you to do something specific for him, you will be close enough to hear his voice and wise enough to respond.

How do I know if I am following God's will?

ESTHER 4:14 | *[Mordecai asked Esther,] "Who knows if perhaps you were made queen for just such a time as this?"*

PSALM 32:8 | *The LORD says, "I will guide you along the best pathway for your life. I will advise you and watch over you."*

PSALM 138:8 | *The LORD will work out his plans for my life.*

PSALM 139:3 | *You see me when I travel and when I rest at home. You know everything I do.*

JEREMIAH 29:11 | *"I know the plans I have for you," says the LORD. "They are plans for good and not for disaster, to give you a future and a hope."*

These Scripture verses, and many more, make it clear that God does have a plan for your life. So how do you know what it is and if you are following it? The first step is simply to accept that God does have a plan for you. Without this first step of faith, you will miss everything God does to get your attention. Next, open your eyes—your spiritual eyes. Notice the people that come into your life, who cross your path during the day. These are potentially people whom God wants to use in your life or to whom he wants you to minister. Act on what and whom God places in front of you and you will follow his plan for your life, day by day, month by month, year by year. Your life will always have a sense of mystery because you don't know the future, but if you act upon each situation God puts in front of you, your life will not seem random nor will it seem like an automated script you must follow. When you are always watching for God's work in your life, you will train yourself to notice these moments orchestrated by God and recognize them for what they are.

WISDOM

How can I obtain more wisdom?

1 KINGS 3:9 | *Give me an understanding heart so that I can . . . know the difference between right and wrong.*

PROVERBS 3:21-24, 26 | *Don't lose sight of common sense and discernment. Hang on to them, for they will refresh your soul. . . . They keep you safe on your way, and your feet will not stumble. You can go to bed without fear; you will lie down and sleep soundly, . . . for the LORD is your security. He will keep your foot from being caught in a trap.*

PROVERBS 9:10 | *Fear of the LORD is the foundation of wisdom. Knowledge of the Holy One results in good judgment.*

ECCLESIASTES 10:10 | *Using a dull ax requires great strength, so sharpen the blade. That's the value of wisdom; it helps you succeed.*

JAMES 1:5 | *If you need wisdom, ask our generous God, and he will give it to you. He will not rebuke you for asking.*

Solving a complex problem in trigonometry or writing a computer program that will guide a nuclear missile requires great intelligence. But such intelligence does not guarantee a fulfilling or productive life. Having success in relationships,

raising godly children, and growing in spiritual maturity
are less dependent on intellect than on wisdom. The Bible
has an enormous amount to say about wisdom (and even
devotes the entire book of Proverbs to it) because successfully
navigating through life requires so much of it. Wisdom recognizes that an all-powerful, all-knowing God has designed a
moral universe with consequences for good or sinful choices.
Wisdom begins with understanding your accountability to
and your full dependence on your Creator—it's not what you
know, but *whom* you know. Wisdom from God helps you
develop a godly outlook that penetrates the deceptive and
distorted thoughts of the world. And wisdom is choosing to
apply God's truth and principles to your daily relationships
and situations, helping you know the difference between
good and bad, right and wrong.

How can I be wise at a moment's notice?

2 TIMOTHY 2:21 | *If you keep yourself pure, you will be a special
utensil for honorable use. Your life will be clean, and you will
be ready for the Master to use you for every good work.*

The key is to prepare yourself by developing wisdom over
time. You do that by keeping yourself "pure," in other
words by filling your mind more with God's words than
the world's advice. You can't always anticipate what might
happen in a day, but when you are prepared spiritually—
when you have developed wisdom—you know the right
things to do in God's eyes. This gives you the courage to act
swiftly and decisively when necessary because you have a
wellspring of wisdom to draw upon.

WITNESSING

How do I tell others about Jesus?

EXODUS 18:8 | *Moses told his father-in-law everything the LORD had done to Pharaoh and Egypt on behalf of Israel. He also told about all the hardships they had experienced along the way and how the LORD had rescued his people from all their troubles.*

PSALM 107:2 | *Has the LORD redeemed you? Then speak out! Tell others he has redeemed you from your enemies.*

MARK 16:15 | *[Jesus said,] "Go into all the world and preach the Good News to everyone."*

ROMANS 10:15 | *How beautiful are the feet of messengers who bring good news!*

2 TIMOTHY 1:7-8 | *God has not given us a spirit of fear and timidity, but of power, love, and self-discipline. So never be ashamed to tell others about our Lord.*

A friend mentions in casual conversation that she enjoyed a terrific meal at a new restaurant and thinks you would like it too. A stranger overhears you and your spouse wondering if a certain movie would be good to rent for a family night, and he offers that his kids thought it was great. Both the friend and the stranger are witnesses. Although the word *witness* brings to mind images of courtrooms or awkward religious proselytizing, to "witness" simply means to tell about something you have experienced. All who believe in God share the privilege and responsibility of witnessing. Believing in God isn't about getting in some exclusive group. It's about experiencing something so wonderful that you can't wait to invite others to experience it as well. It's the practice of sharing your spiritual story with others. You should always be ready to tell the story of how you met and grew to love Jesus. That story is the greatest story you could tell. Who knows? Perhaps sharing your own story will be the pathway to a divine moment in another's life.

PHILIPPIANS 4:8-9 | *Fix your thoughts on what is true, and honorable, and right, and pure, and lovely, and admirable. Think about things that are excellent and worthy of praise. Keep putting into practice all you learned. . . . Then the God of peace will be with you.*

TITUS 2:7-8 | *You . . . must be an example . . . by doing good works of every kind. Let everything you do reflect the integrity and seriousness of your teaching. Teach the truth so that your teaching can't be criticized. Then those who oppose us will be ashamed and have nothing bad to say about us.*

1 PETER 3:15-16 | *You must worship Christ as Lord of your life. And if someone asks about your Christian hope, always be ready to explain it. But do this in a gentle and respectful way. Keep your conscience clear. Then if people speak against you, they will be ashamed when they see what a good life you live because you belong to Christ.*

One way to effectively witness to others is to do your best to live like Jesus did. Then people will start to notice what makes you different and why you have a unique passion and purpose for life. They will be drawn to God's Spirit active within you and will want to know how they can live that way.

WORDS

Why are profanity and coarse words such a big deal? They're just words.

PHILIPPIANS 4:8 | *Fix your thoughts on what is true, and honorable, and right, and pure, and lovely, and admirable. Think about things that are excellent and worthy of praise.*

JAMES 1:26 | *If you claim to be religious but don't control your tongue, you are fooling yourself, and your religion is worthless.*

What comes out of your mouth shows what is in your heart. Your words show what kind of person you really are. Criticism, gossip, flattery, lies, and profanity are not only word problems but heart problems as well. Being more careful with your words isn't enough. You must first have a change of heart, and then good, kind, and healing words will follow.

EPHESIANS 4:29 | *Don't use foul or abusive language. Let everything you say be good and helpful, so that your words will be an encouragement to those who hear them.*

What kind of an impact could you have on others if you replaced all your negative or unhelpful words with words of kindness, encouragement, and gratitude?

PSALM 15:1-3 | *Who may worship in your sanctuary, LORD? Who may enter your presence on your holy hill? Those who lead blameless lives and do what is right, speaking the truth from sincere hearts. Those who refuse to gossip or harm their neighbors or speak evil of their friends.*

You wouldn't give an obscene gift to the president, or even to a friend, and it would certainly be a bad idea to give an insulting gift to an enemy. Your words are no different. In fact, the greatest gift you will ever give others is not in a box covered with paper and a bow, but in the words you use to encourage, inspire, comfort, and challenge them. Don't let your words be annoying, insulting, demeaning, or simply useless. Because they show the kind of person you really are, make your words truly matter.

WORK

What if my work has nothing to do with anything "Christian"—how can God be glorified in my work?

GENESIS 2:2 | *On the seventh day God had finished his work of creation, so he rested from all his work.*

GENESIS 2:15 | *The LORD God placed the man in the Garden of Eden to tend and watch over it.*

COLOSSIANS 3:23 | *Work willingly at whatever you do, as though you were working for the Lord rather than for people.*

1 THESSALONIANS 4:11-12 | *Make it your goal to live a quiet life, minding your own business and working with your hands, just as we instructed you before. Then people who are not Christians will respect the way you live, and you will not need to depend on others.*

2 THESSALONIANS 3:8 | *We worked hard day and night so we would not be a burden to any of you.*

Work is anchored in God's very character. Part of being made in God's image is sharing in the industrious and creative aspects of his nature. Animal husbandry and gardening, for example, were the very first jobs given to humans. Christians are needed in all kinds of vocations. Whatever your job, believe that God has placed you there for a reason, and then do your work well as a service to him and as a way to serve others. Then, when someone asks you why you work hard and strive for excellence, you can explain exactly why.

WORSHIP

What is worship?

1 CHRONICLES 29:10-13 | *David praised the LORD in the presence of the whole assembly: "O LORD, the God of our ancestor Israel, may you be praised forever and ever! Yours, O LORD, is the greatness, the power, the glory, the victory, and the majesty. Everything in the heavens and on earth is yours, O LORD, and this is your kingdom. We adore you as the one who is over all things. Wealth and honor come from you alone, for you rule over everything. Power and might are in your hand, and at your discretion people are made great and given strength. O our God, we thank you and praise your glorious name!"*

ROMANS 11:33-36 | *Oh, how great are God's riches and wisdom and knowledge! How impossible it is for us to understand his decisions and his ways! For who can know the LORD's thoughts? Who knows enough to give him advice? And who has given him so much that he needs to pay it back? For everything comes from him and exists by his power and is intended for his glory. All glory to him forever! Amen.*

PHILIPPIANS 2:9-11 | *God elevated [Jesus] to the place of highest honor and gave him the name above all other names, that at the name of Jesus every knee should bow, in heaven and on earth and under the earth, and every tongue confess that Jesus Christ is Lord, to the glory of God the Father.*

Human beings were created to worship. Worshiping is ascribing ultimate value to an object, a person, or God— and then to revere, adore, pay homage to, and obey by ordering the priorities of your life around that which you worship. The Bible teaches that God alone is worthy of your worship. Ultimately, everything you do should be based on what you think of and how you worship the almighty God. If your actions don't give ultimate honor to him, then you are worshiping someone or something else. Worship, more than anything else, will connect you with God, your only source of lasting hope and joy.

How is worship integral to my relationship with God? Why is it important?

EXODUS 34:8 | *Moses immediately threw himself to the ground and worshiped.*

1 CHRONICLES 16:29 | *Give to the LORD the glory he deserves! Bring your offering and come into his presence. Worship the LORD in all his holy splendor.*

PSALM 145:3 | *Great is the LORD! He is most worthy of praise! No one can measure his greatness.*

ISAIAH 66:1-2 | *This is what the LORD says: "Heaven is my throne, and the earth is my footstool. Could you build me a temple as good as that? Could you build me such a resting place? My hands have made both heaven and earth; they and everything in them are mine. I, the LORD, have spoken! I will bless those who have humble and contrite hearts, who tremble at my word."*

Worship is the recognition of who God is and who you are in relation to him. It is recognizing his gracious character and his many acts of love toward you, and then returning love to him.

PSALM 5:7 | *Because of your unfailing love, I can enter your house; I will worship at your Temple with deepest awe.*

ISAIAH 6:3 | *Holy, holy, holy is the LORD of Heaven's Armies! The whole earth is filled with his glory!*

Worship is a fitting response to God's holiness, power, love, and grace.

DEUTERONOMY 31:11 | *You must read this Book of Instruction to all the people of Israel when they assemble before the LORD your God at the place he chooses.*

PSALM 150:3-5 | *Praise [God] with a blast of the ram's horn; praise him with the lyre and harp! Praise him with the tambourine and dancing; praise him with strings and flutes! Praise him with a clash of cymbals; praise him with loud clanging cymbals.*

ACTS 2:46-47 | *[All the believers] worshiped together at the Temple each day, met in homes for the Lord's Supper, and shared their meals with great joy and generosity—all the while praising God and enjoying the goodwill of all the people. And each day the Lord added to their fellowship those who were being saved.*

ROMANS 15:5-6 | *May God, who gives this patience and encouragement, help you live in complete harmony with each other, as is fitting for followers of Christ Jesus. Then all of you can join together with one voice, giving praise and glory to God, the Father of our Lord Jesus Christ.*

EPHESIANS 4:16 | *[Christ] makes the whole body fit together perfectly. As each part does its own special work, it helps the other parts grow, so that the whole body is healthy and growing and full of love.*

EPHESIANS 5:18-19 | *Be filled with the Holy Spirit, singing psalms and hymns and spiritual songs among yourselves, and making music to the Lord in your hearts.*

Something unique happens when God's people congregate to sing, praise, and listen to his Word, worshiping him together. There is a sense of community and fellowship that can happen only when believers worship together.

What does worshiping God involve? How should I worship him?

EXODUS 20:2-3 | *I am the LORD your God, who rescued you from the land of Egypt, the place of your slavery. You must not have any other god but me.*

DEUTERONOMY 11:16 | *Be careful. Don't let your heart be deceived so that you turn away from the LORD and serve and worship other gods.*

PSALM 96:4 | *Great is the LORD! He is most worthy of praise! He is to be feared above all gods.*

REVELATION 22:9 | *[The angel] said, "No, don't worship me. I am a servant of God, just like you and your brothers the prophets, as well as all who obey what is written in this book. Worship only God!"*

Worship only God, because he alone is worthy of your utmost devotion.

EXODUS 3:5 | *"Do not come any closer," the LORD warned. "Take off your sandals, for you are standing on holy ground."*

When you approach God's presence in worship, recognize that, wherever you are, you are standing on holy ground. In other words, come to almighty God with an attitude of humility and respect for him.

PSALM 9:11 | *Sing praises to the LORD. . . . Tell the world about his unforgettable deeds.*

PSALM 35:18 | *[O Lord,] I will thank you in front of the great assembly. I will praise you before all the people.*

HEBREWS 13:15 | *Let us offer through Jesus a continual sacrifice of praise to God, proclaiming our allegiance to his name.*

Your worship should include praise and thanks to God for what he has done.

1 CHRONICLES 15:16 | *David . . . ordered the Levite leaders to appoint a choir of Levites who were singers and musicians to sing joyful songs to the accompaniment of harps, lyres, and cymbals.*

PSALM 147:1 | *Praise the LORD! How good to sing praises to our God! How delightful and how fitting!*

PSALM 150:3-5 | *Praise [God] with a blast of the ram's horn; praise him with the lyre and harp! Praise him with the tambourine and dancing; praise him with strings and flutes! Praise him with a clash of cymbals; praise him with loud clanging cymbals.*

EPHESIANS 5:19 | *[Sing] psalms and hymns and spiritual songs among yourselves, and [make] music to the Lord in your hearts.*

Worship can take the form of music with instruments and singing.

WORTH

What am I worth—what is my value to God?

GENESIS 1:27 | *God created human beings in his own image. In the image of God he created them; male and female he created them.*

PSALM 8:5 | *[The Lord] made [human beings] only a little lower than God and crowned them with glory and honor.*

MATTHEW 16:26 | *What do you benefit if you gain the whole world but lose your own soul? Is anything worth more than your soul?*

EPHESIANS 2:10 | *We are God's masterpiece. He has created us anew in Christ Jesus, so we can do the good things he planned for us long ago.*

God made you in his own image, so he must value you highly! You are his treasure and masterpiece!

1 CORINTHIANS 7:23 | *God paid a high price for you, so don't be enslaved by the world.*

You are worthy because God paid a high price for you. He loved you enough to offer his only Son, Jesus, as a sacrifice for you. You are invaluable to him, which is why he sent his own Son to die for your sins so that you could live in heaven with him forever. That's how important you are to him!

EPHESIANS 1:4-7 | *Even before he made the world, God loved us and chose us in Christ to be holy and without fault in his eyes. God decided in advance to adopt us into his own family by bringing us to himself through Jesus Christ. This is what he wanted to do, and it gave him great pleasure. So we praise God for the glorious grace he has poured out on us who belong to his dear Son. He is so rich in kindness and grace that he purchased our freedom with the blood of his Son and forgave our sins.*

Before God made the world, he chose you to be born as his unique creation, and he has done the work to make you holy and forgiven. Have you accepted what he has done for you? If not, wouldn't you like to do so now?

new believer's

Go Deeper with the *New Believer's Bible*.

BIBLE

The *New Believer's Bible* is uniquely designed to help the new Christian read, study, and understand the Bible. It includes features that help Christians develop and deepen their faith, while providing a foundation for their new life in Christ.

Features and benefits:
- Clear and accurate New Living Translation
- Four Reading Tracks: Cornerstones, First Steps, Off and Running, and Big Questions
- How You Can Know God
- How to Study the Bible
- One Year New Testament Reading Plan
- 52 Great Bible Stories
- Memory Verses
- Prophecies about Jesus
- Glossary of Christian Terms
- Book Introductions